The History of the Pneumatic Tyre

Eric Tompkins

John Boyd Dunlop 1840-1921

The History of the Pneumatic Tyre

Eric Tompkins

Produced by the
Dunlop Archive Project
and published by the
Eastland Press

ISBN No. 0 903214 14 8

Printed at The Lavenham Press Limited, Suffolk.
Binding by Norton Bridge Bookbinders Ltd.
Lithographic separation and specialised typesetting from
Star Illustration, London.
Illustrations and Diagrams by Robin Griggs and Tony Simmonds
Endpiece Vignettes by Peter Stevenson, R.C.A.
Design by Harriet Wylie, R.C.A.
Produced and Edited by Derek Green.

Author's Acknowledgements

When I first went to work at Fort Dunlop, in 1927, Bob Carlisle was a member of the Accounts Department and was proud that he was a link with J. B. Dunlop, having been a rider in the cycle race in Belfast, in 1889, when W. Hume scored the first win on the new pneumatic tyre.

When I retired, 42 years later, it was one of my ambitions to write a record of the development of the pneumatic tyre, from the very beginning down to the present day. This book is the result. It does not claim to be encyclopedic; much is left out and few names are recorded, but looking back at the story I feel fortunate to have been able to set down so much of the thread of the history, which might otherwise have been broken or lost.

Theseus, in Shakespeare's 'Midsummer Night's Dream', reminds us how 'imagination bodies forth the forms of things unknown'. Thomson's invention and Dunlop's timely reinvention were examples of this use of imagination, to produce a completely new idea, of great use to mankind. For the rest, let the words and the pictures speak for themselves.

I owe deep thanks to Dunlop Limited for keeping the idea of this book alive through the changes and chances of recent years. I am grateful to Sir Campbell Fraser for his personal interest and for his most kind Foreword.

Along the trail of the production of the book there are many people I should thank. To single out individuals would be invidious, but most names appear at one place or another in either credits or the acknowledgements.

Any reader who is able and willing to add to our knowledge of tyre history is invited to write up his story, which will be gratefully received by the Archive Project.

Formal thanks are given to H.M. Patent Office for the drawings in Figures 1.2-1.5 and 10.4, and to the Science Museum for Figure 2.5 of the Dunlop tyre in their collection.

E. S. Tompkins.

Contents

INDEX

Illustrations

All illustrations are the copyright of Dunlop Limited unless otherwise credited.

Introduction
by Sir Campbell Fraser

I have a clear memory of Eric Tompkins introducing me to the technical mysteries of the pneumatic tyre. "In essence", he said "you are looking at 2½ ounces of a compressible, deformable material, in the form of air, contained within a rubberized flexible envelope. The combination of these two parts, and their individual characteristics working separately or in unison, enable the pneumatic tyre to perform the functions required of it by a vehicle". That was, of course, just the starting point of my education in such matters. But the beautiful simplicity of explanation typifies the clarity with which Eric can communicate the most important fundamentals as a base from which to take you forward into the complexities which inevitably follow.

The history of the pneumatic tyre is indeed a story, albeit of true life. Eric Tompkins belongs to a generation who entered the tyre business when the pioneers were still around to recount the events of the early days. He played a part in the transformation of a business into an industry in its own right, saw technology replace rule of thumb and craft, and contributed to the applied sciences of the early sixties. Today he still has a direct involvement in many matters appertaining to the world of the tyre.

Both during his career in the industry and subsequently, Eric, as an experienced writer, was a regular contributor to journals and trade magazines. It is indeed fortunate that someone of his generation and experience should have put down on paper, as a permanent record, his unrivalled knowledge of the development of the pneumatic tyre; a story which in many ways reflects the social and business history of the past ninety years.

Campbell Fraser

Dunlop House
May 1981

Chairman, Dunlop Holdings Limited

CHAPTER 1

Invention

Inventions are of two kinds. The simplest is mere makeshift improvisation, such as gave rise to the old proverb which names necessity as the mother of invention. An inventor, faced with the man who had lost his teeth, is prompted to devise makeshift teeth, to restore the ability to chew food. The need is there and the invention merely copies, with as much skill as is available, the form and the way of working of the missing teeth.

On a much higher plane, the true inventor produces, from the depths of his imagination, something hitherto completely unknown. This was true of the first invention of the pneumatic tyre, in 1845. One day no-one had ever thought of anything like an inflated tube, fixed round the rim of a wheel. The next day, through the exercise of the inventor's imagination, the idea was born, and the world was the richer for the acquisition of a completely new device.

The first recorded inventor of the pneumatic tyre was Robert William Thomson, who was born in Stonehouse, Kincardineshire, Scotland, on the 29 June, 1822, the son of a small factory owner. His parents hoped that Robert might become a minister of the church, but the boy had other ideas. At the age of fourteen he was sent to Charleston, U.S.A., to be educated as a merchant. Instead he attached himself to an engineer, some say to a smith, and received practical training in that direction. When he came back to Scotland, two years later, he was employed in workshops in Dundee and Aberdeen, and spent some time working for Robert Stevenson, the famous civil engineer.

R. W. Thomson

In 1844, at the age of 22, he was in business on his own account as a railway engineer, with an office in Adam Street, in London, off the Strand. It was here that the great invention of the pneumatic tyre was worked out (Figure 1·1).

The diagram (Figure 1·2) is taken from the patent specification, No 10,990, finally dated the 10 June 1846. The first operative

The first patent, 1845

1

sentence in the description which goes with them shows that Thomson, unlike some inventors, knew exactly what he was attempting to do. It reads: '*The nature of my said Invention consists in the application of elastic bearings round the tires of the wheels of carriages, for the purpose of lessening the power required to draw the carriages, rendering their motion easier and diminishing the noise they make when in motion.*' Seldom have three such good ideas been expressed in forty-six words, in any patent application, before or since that date.

Thomson's patent is a highly intelligent document. It sets out in exact detail how the invention is to be constructed and what materials are recommended for use in making it. The inventor is remarkably up to date in his technology. Vulcanisation, the process of stabilising rubber by compounding it with sulphur and heating the mixture, was discovered only in 1839, while Thomson was still in America, yet it is mentioned here in the patent specification as a process suitable for use in the manufacture of the aerial wheel, and capable of affecting its design.

The Aerial Wheel

Let us now look at the way in which the new tyre, which Thomson called the Aerial Wheel, was to be made. The fundamental part of it was described in the specification as '*a hollow belt, composed of some air- and water-tight material, such as caoutchouc (rubber) or gutta-percha, (inflated) with air, whereby the wheels will in every part of their revolution present a cushion of air to the ground or rail or track on which they run.*' Thomson's work as a railway engineer can be seen in this description—he was thinking as much of applications on the railways as on the road.

Construction

The diagram (Figure 1·3), shows the construction of the Aerial Wheel, based on the experiments which Thomson had already carried out. The wheel is that of a horse-drawn cart or carriage. The new tyre is super-imposed on the existing construction of the iron-shod wheel, with its wooden spokes, slotted into a wooden felloe, held together by a shrunk-on iron tyre.

The Aerial wheel itself is made in two parts. The inner tube is shown as built up from rubbered canvas. The patent reads: '*A number of folds of canvas, saturated and covered on both sides with india rubber or gutta percha, in a state of solution, are laid one upon the other, and each fold connected to the one immediately below it by a solution of india rubber or gutta percha, or other suitable cement.*'

The outer cover, as shown in the diagrams and explained in the text,

2

consists of segments of leather. The method of building up the structure from such segments, and of rivetting them together and bolting the whole tyre on to the rim, is shown in detail in the drawings.

This seems to have been the way in which the first prototypes of the new tyre were made. It is plain to see that the construction started with the idea of a leather casing, which had the required resistance to wear and flexing. Having decided on this part of the structure, and knowing that leather stretched when wet, and would become distended by the internal pressure in the tyre, it is easy to see why the inner tube had to be reinforced with canvas.

Thomson's patent is full of farsightedness. He sees the advantage of vulcanising the tube with sulphur and, in what was obviously an addition to the original draft, he sketches out ways of vulcanising the original canvas reinforced tube, or of making the outer cover itself of such material. '. . . . *or the belt* (*tube*) *may be made of a single thickness of rubber or gutta percha, in a sheet state and sulphurised as aforesaid, and then enclosed in a canvas cover.*'

Thomson's Vision

The patent then describes the valve through which the tyre is inflated, and we begin to see the trained engineer thinking over the new device which he has created, and seeing more and more possibilities.

First, he suggests that inflation shall be with air, '*as being more suitable than anything else for the purpose*'. But he goes on to suggest that the new tyre might be filled with '*various solid substances of an elastic quality, as for instance metallic springs, sulphurised pieces of caoutchouc or gutta percha, or horse hair or sponge. If the elastic belt were first stuffed with horse hair or sponge, or other elastic materials, and then inflated by blowing in air to a high degree of tension, the belt would be less likely to be cut by concussion between the tire of the wheel and the roadway.*' This prophetic suggestion to use inflated natural sponge as a tyre filler has come to pass 120 years later, in the experiments carried out in the U.S.A. in which inflated synthetic foams have been cast inside fitted tyre and wheel assemblies.

The specification then goes on to show how completely the idea of the aerial wheel had taken possession of the young inventor's mind. A wealth of ideas come tumbling out and are all written down as possible further developments of the basic inflated tyre. Most of them have subsequently been realised.

First, the idea of a tyre containing multiple tubes is well developed. He suggests a group of nine of these multiple tubes (Figure 1·4), inside

3

the cover, and that they might be run at differential pressures, with the innermost ones, those in contact with the rim, at higher pressures than those in contact, through the tread, with the ground. He also suggests tieing the tubes at intervals, sausage fashion, so that any puncture damage shall be restricted in its effect to a small part of the circumference of the wheel. Both these suggestions seem to be in terms of reinforced fabric tubes, where ballooning under pressure is restrained.

The patent goes on to explore various advantages of the segmental build-up of the outer leather cover. The rivetted construction, with joints round the mid-wall of the tyre, enables the tread portion to be replaced when worn or damaged. In the alternative build-up, with a circumferential joint round the centreline of the tread, the inventor sees the rivets as an anti-skid or road-gripping device, such as became available to the motorist only since the appearance of tungsten-carbide ice-studs.

Railway uses

Next comes a section of the specification which shows the young railway engineer adapting the Aerial wheel to his own field. The application suggested is to what he describes as timber railways, on which ordinary road carts, with iron-shod wheels, run on planks forming wooden 'lines', the trucks being kept on the track by continuous up-standing guide rails, also of wood (Figure 1·5). Illustrations are given of pneumatic tyres being operated in this way. The final thought is that the driving wheels of the locomotive might be equipped with tyres, having rivets in their treads with sharp conical heads, to increase the bite of the drive on the wooden rails. He comments on the advantages to be gained by the use of such a tyre and goes on to suggest that the use of it might *enable steam carriages to run on common roads, with great advantage both for carrying passengers and goods.*

His final paragraph, on other possible developments of the Aerial wheel, shows how completely the invention had captured his mind, and how far he could see into its future development. He suggests that his 'elastic bearings' might be fitted to bath chairs and even to the rockers of rocking-chairs. There is a touch of prophesy too in the suggestion that the inflated bearing principle should be applied to furnish rollers for moving heavy bodies. The engineer in Thomson visualises such rollers, with inflated surfaces, *'so that a large number of them may be made to bear equally at the same time, even though the ways on which the body is being moved are not quite even.'* Here we

4

may see in Thomson's idea the basic principle of inflated lifting-bags which are now used in salvaging heavy aircraft from landings on soft terrain.

Does the invention work? Thomson wanted an answer to this question for his Aerial wheel, and he set to finding out in a practical way. A year after the filing of his patent, he equipped a horse-drawn brougham with aerial wheels, of the later type with rubbered canvas outer covers, and carried out some tests in Regents Park, measuring the force required to draw the vehicle along. The results were published in The Mechanic's Magazine, Vol. 50, in 1849, together with a drawing of the carriage (Figure 1·6). The figures are striking, showing a 38% reduction in the pull required on the waterbound Macadam (no stone bigger than you could put into your mouth, was the instruction of Macadam to his workmen); and 68% reduction in pull on the newly-laid broken flints. Thus the tests were notably successful and the account in the magazine paid special tribute to the silence, comfort and easy running of the vehicle on the new wheels, and commented on the absence of any signs of wear on the tread of the tyres during the experiments.

So there it was. One of the major inventions of a highly inventive age; thought out, proven and ready for development. Unhappily, it rested there. No-one came forward to pick up the idea and develop it to the stage where the new wheels could be produced in large quantities, at a price which would be attractive to the many users of horse-drawn carriages.

The wonderful invention languished unused. Thomson went out to Java, as an engineer, where he was concerned with the installation of machinery on sugar plantations. During his ten years there he continued to invent, in a broad field, with designs for a steam crane and for a floating dock. In 1862 he returned to Edinburgh where, in 1867, he took out a patent for a wide solid rubber tyre, for use on a heavy road steam vehicle of tricycle design. This vehicle travelled at over 20 m.p.h. and was said by The Scotsman, in June 1870, to herald 'a new era in locomotion as far as our large towns and public roads are concerned.'

In spite of this interest in solid tyres for his heavy vehicles, the inventor still used Aerial wheels on his personal carriage and there is a record of him demonstrating these tyres to the Emperor of Brazil, who visited Edinburgh to see the road-steamer, in 1869.

Testing

Stagnation

5

Robert Thomson died in 1873, at the age of fifty-one, following a few years beset with illness. After his death the Aerial wheel was forgotten, although specimens of the invention were preserved in museums (Figure 1·7).

Fifteen years later the idea was to be invented all over again, by another Scot, who had been only five years old at the time of Thomson's original invention.

CHAPTER 2

Re-invention

In 1888 the idea of the pneumatic tyre was invented again, but this time it came under more favourable auspices to a world which may be said to have been waiting on tiptoe for its discovery. The new inventor was John Boyd Dunlop, whose name is known world wide as the man who was responsible for the pneumatic tyre.

Dunlop was born at Dreghorn, in Ayrshire, in south-west Scotland, on 5 February 1840, the son of a tenant-farmer. He studied in Edinburgh, finishing his training at the Royal Dick Veterinary College. In his early twenties he migrated to northern Ireland, setting up practices first in Kirkpatrick and later in Belfast, where the size of his establishment was such that he employed twelve horseshoers (Figure 2·1).

J. B. Dunlop

When his son Johnnie was ten, the boy appealed to his father for some device to make his solid-tyred tricycle run more smoothly and faster on the granite setts and tramlines of the city streets.

The details of the first experiments are well documented. Dunlop built up a pneumatic tyre, of rubbered canvas, enclosing a rubber tube, round the periphery of a wooden disc. This model tyre was inflated with air (Figure 2·2). The first simple experiment was made to compare its liveliness with that of the small-section solid tyre, on the front wheel of the tricycle. This wheel was removed from the machine, and Dunlop invited his assistants and his family to watch a rolling test, in which the two wheels were bowled along the floor of the yard at the Dunlop house.

Experiments

The solid tyred wheel from the tricycle went first. Rolled with an underarm movement, it ran along the paved yard, until all the energy, with which it had been propelled, had been used up, when it wobbled to a standstill and fell down. Next the wooden disc with the air tyre was rolled in the same way and with the same force. This bounded along the whole length of the yard, hit the closed doors at the far

7

end, and rebounded, with energy still stored within it.

This was the basic experiment, much cruder than the tests with the brougham which Thomson had made, but showing unmistakably that the thinking was right and that an air tyre of this kind had something to offer which would be beneficial to the bicycle and to its riders.

The next step was to make a pair of wheels, with pneumatic tyres, and to fit them over the solid tyres on the rear axle of the tricycle. These tyres were built up on wooden rims, made of strips of American elm. On these the canvas covers, with their inner tubes of rubber and outer tread of layers of rubber sheeting, were built up, and tacked in place round the edges of the wooden strips. These rims were then slipped over the outsides of the solid tyres on the tricycle, and bound into position for the test. Simple inflation tubes, like those used in a football, were used for filling the tyres with air and retaining it (Figure 2·3).

Work, involving the building up of articles from rubber sheeting, with rubber solution and canvas, was not new to Dunlop. He had much practice in building up various devices required in his veterinary work.

Road tests

The tricycle was tried out on the road, secretly at night, on 28 February 1888. The run was interrupted by an eclipse of the moon, during which Johnnie returned home, going out again afterwards, about 11 p.m. to complete the test. The next morning, the tyres were examined with some anxiety, for cuts or other damage by the stones which were plentiful on the roads of those days; but no injuries were found. The boy's report on the performance of the machine on its new tyres was most encouraging and gave great hope for the future.

The 'Mummy' tyre

The next stage was to equip a bicycle front and rear, with the new tyre, and to try it out properly. The makeshift construction, using the wooden rims with the edges of the cover tacked in position, was abandoned. The tyre was built up in position on the wire-spoked rim of the actual cycle wheel. The way in which the layers of rubbered sailcloth, which made up the casing of the tyre, were wrapped through the gaps between the spokes of the wire wheel, gave it the name of the 'mummy tyre' (Figure 2·4). The special wheels were made up by a local Belfast cycle maker, Edlin & Co. The bicycle was actually ridden on these prototype tyres for 2000 miles, one of the original pair being still inflated at the end.

A tyre from this earliest period of Dunlop's reinvention is in the

Figure 1.1, above
R. W. Thomson, 1822-1873, inventor of the pneumatic tyre.

Figure 1.2, below
Drawing of the construction of the Aerial Wheel, taken from the Patent Specification of 1845.

Figure 1.3, right
The construction of Thomson's Aerial Wheel, as applied to the wheel of a carriage or cart.

Figure 1.4, below right
The inventor's suggested multiple-tube development of the Aerial Wheel.

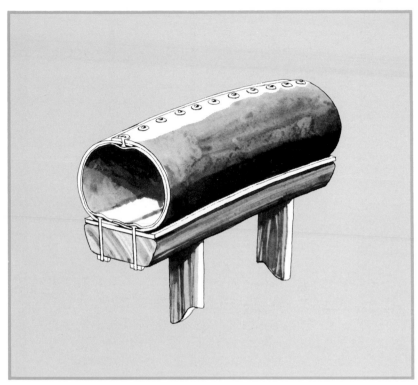

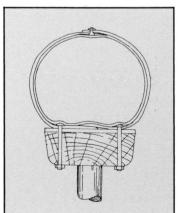

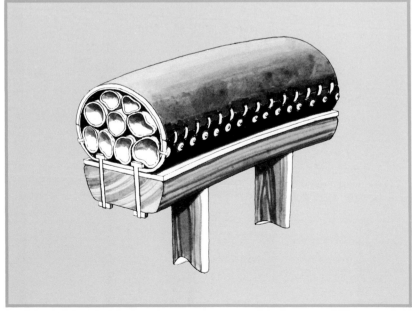

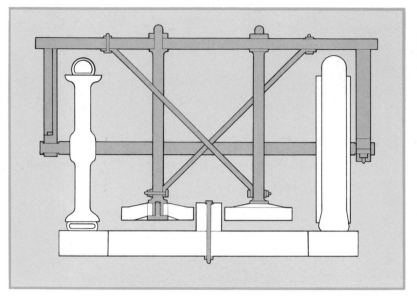

Figure 1.5
From Thomson's Patent. Suggested application of the Aerial wheel to timber track railways. The pneumatic tyre is shown in use on the main load-carrying wheels, which run on flat board tracks. The train is kept on the rails by small steel wheels which run horizontally and engage a central upstanding locating beam.

Figure 1.6
Test results on the Aerial wheels. The improvement in the force required to pull the carriage is striking, even if Messrs. Whitehurst and the Patentee did not really understand how to work out the percentage savings!

Mechanics' Magazine,

MUSEUM, REGISTER, JOURNAL, AND GAZETTE.

No. 1233.] SATURDAY, MARCH 27. [Price 3*d*.

Edited by J. C. Robertson, 166, Fleet-street.

THOMSON'S PATENT AERIAL WHEELS.
Fig. 1.

Result of Experiments tried by Messrs. Whitehurst and Co., and the Patentee, for ascertaining the comparative Draught of R. W. Thomson's Patent Aerial Wheels and the common Wheels. Tried in Regent's Park, March 17, 1847.

Weight of Carriage, 10½ cwts.	Common Wheels. Actual draught in pounds.	Patent Wheels. Actual draught in pounds.	Saving of draught by Patent Wheels,
Over a smooth, hard, macadamized level road	45	28	60 per cent.
Over new broken flints	120	38½	310 per cent.

Figure 1.7, below.
Examples of the Thomson Aerial wheels.

Figure 2.1, right.
J. B. Dunlop's veterinary establishment in Belfast. The yard shown was the scene of the first experiments on the properties of the pneumatic cycle tyre.
Figure 2.2, below right.
Experiments with the model wheel. (Reconstruction.)
Figure 2.3, extreme right.
The tricycle with pneumatic tyres fitted to the rear wheels. (Reconstruction.)

Below. Johnnie Dunlop

Figure 2.4, right.
The construction of the Dunlop 'mummy' tyre.
Figure 2.5.
Original Dunlop 'mummy' tyre in the Science Museum, South Kensington.

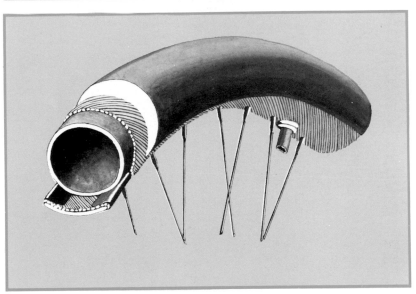

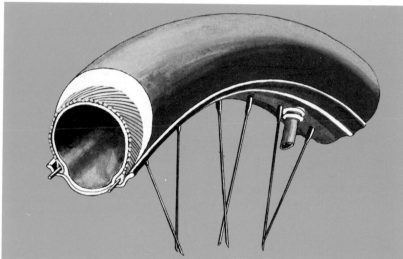

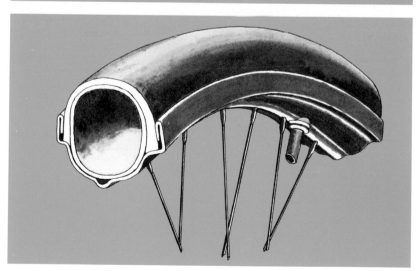

Left.
The Tubular tyre, (see p.9).

Figure 2.7, below left
The Welch wire-type tyre, with well-base rim.

Figure 2.6, below
J. B. Dunlop (1840-1921), with his family at about the time of the reinvention of the pneumatic tyre.

Figure 2.8, left
The Bartlett beaded edge tyre, as described in the patent.

Figure 2.9, below
The Bartlett tyre modified with bead and rim hooked, to give a positive action.

Science Museum at South Kensington, London (Figure 2·5). This exhibit is in a somewhat decrepit state, as the years have led to much ageing of the rubber forming the tread and wall. Such exhibits are often disappointing and it needs some imagination to visualise them as they were in their pristine state, when this tattered old tyre was new and spruce and represented the beginning of a new industry and a new era in transport.

The reasoning behind Dunlop's invention was exactly the same as that which prompted Thomson, forty-three years earlier, but this time the situation in the world had changed, the bicycle had arrived, and there was a market waiting for the new device.

J. B. Dunlop followed up his first patent with two others on the pneumatic tyre. These were dated 8 March 1889 and covered a form of valve to replace the crude devices which had been used in the earlier stages. By this time other inventors were working in the tyre field and, only four days after Dunlop's second patent, A. T. Thomas filed a specification, covering an arched inflated tyre, with several mechanical methods of fastening it to the rim.

More patents

During this same period, there was interest in what are called 'tubular tyres'. In such designs, the cover and the tube are made in one endless hoop and the complete tyre is solutioned or otherwise attached to a rim of suitable concave profile, designed to accept it. This type of tyre persisted for a long time in America and elsewhere, especially as it was clear of the patents which restricted the subsequent development of other kinds of detachable tyres.

Tubular tyres

There are very few photographs of John Boyd Dunlop, and still fewer that do him justice. Most of the stock pictures, which are brought out from time to time, are of a man in his seventies, usually astride some primitive bicycle, in a parade of veterans of the industry. Such pictures do not represent him in the years in which he re-invented the pneumatic tyre. The family group (Figure 2·6), shows him in those days, the vigorous forty-year-old, in the prime of manhood.

It is useful to note how Dunlop's rediscovery of the tyre fits into the history of the bicycle itself. Here are the main dates:

The man and the machine

1818   The hobby-horse, without pedals and propelled by the feet on the ground, brought up to date and popularised by Baron von Drais.

1839   Bicycle, with rear wheels driven through rods by 'treadles'; inventor Kirkpatrick Macmillan.

1863   Michaud, father and son, introduce the velocipede or 'boneshaker', with direct drive through pedals on the front spindle.

1872   The 'penny-farthing' or 'ordinary' bicycle designed by James Starley the elder of Coventry.

1885   The Rover safety cycle, with diamond frame and rear wheel drive, invented by J. K. Starley.

It will be seen that the reinvention of the pneumatic tyre, by Dunlop, came at the very peak of the sixty years development of the bicycle.

The tyre and racing

It is striking that the advantages of the pneumatic tyre were appreciated so quickly, not just as a novelty, but as a new departure with real demonstrable advantages. The new tyre found its way on to racing cycles when it was only about a year old; in fact less than six months after the publication of Dunlop's patent. Its first appearance on any track was at the Queen's College Sports, in Belfast, in June 1889. Here, fitted to the safety bicycle of William Hume, the new tyres were run against the racers of the day on their solid-tyred 'ordinaries'. Although Hume is described as only a 'medium rider', he won all three of the races which he entered, defeating an opposition which, on paper, was much stronger. He also weathered opposition from the derision of the crowd, who laughed at his pudding tyres or bolsters, as they were called.

These victories for the new tyre, on its first outing, excited public interest, so that the Belfast firm of Edlin & Co. quickly sold fifty bicycles with the new tyres to local customers. It should be stressed that this was still the tyre in its crudest prototype form, the 'mummy' tyre, still wrapped in between the spokes of the wire wheel, so as to enclose the rim in its windings, and made of makeshift materials under the supervision of the inventor himself.

Commercial development

The racing successes spread the news that there was a new kind of tyre available for bicycles, and that it had striking new properties. The commercial development of the invention began with the setting up of a small company in Dublin, late in 1889, under the name of The Pneumatic Tyre and Booth's Cycle Agency Limited, with a capital of £25,000. The company was based on Booth's Cycle Agency, who were importers of all the best English makes of machine. Edlin and Findlay Sinclair, of the Edlin firm, who had been building prototype bicycles for pneumatic tyres, were taken over by the new company.

The prospectus, drawn up by the Chairman, Harvey du Cros, was short but enthusiastic, as the following extract shows: '*The advantages which accrue from the use of this tyre upon a roadster cannot be fully understood except by a personal trial. Vibration, with the consequent nervous exhaustion, which tells more against a rider in the course of a long journey than even physical fatigue, is practically annihilated. All vibration is intercepted between the rim and the ground, and consequently the frame of the machine receives no jar, and will last much longer than the frame of the machine fitted with solid tyres. As a result of this, riders will be able to use lighter frames, with a corresponding increase of speed and ease of propulsion. This, taken in conjunction with the absence of nervous exhaustion, and the conservation of power through the machine getting over rough surfaces unchecked, will, it is believed, place the pneumatic tyred machine beyond the reach of competition.*'

This extract emphasises the extent to which the intrinsic technical merit of the pneumatic principle was appreciated by du Cros and the team who were helping him to launch the new company. The tyre itself was still extremely crude in its design, and had to be fitted to the wheel, wrapped between the spokes and solutioned in place.

A month after the formation of the company, a group of important Coventry cycle manufacturers asked for licences for the supply and fixing of pneumatic tyres. After consideration, the Pneumatic Tyre Company decided not to licence in this way but to throw the supply of tyres open to the trade as a whole.

This is no place to write of the commercial birth pangs of the company, or of much of its subsequent development. There are, however, few companies better served in the way of a record of their early growth, written by one of the founders, than is the Dunlop organisation. The book is 'Wheels of Fortune', written by Sir Arthur du Cros, and published in 1938, at the time of the Jubilee of the company. When it appeared there were a few who felt hurt by its record of their part in the history of the half century. This perhaps is inevitable in such circumstances. But as a collection of documented recollections, by the son of the founder of the company, himself its managing director for many years, du Cros's book is a magnificent record. Those who are interested in the commercial growth of the pneumatic tyre industry in England may be able to seek out a copy in libraries with a specific reference section devoted to transport.

The technical side of the story continues with the emergence of two

'Wheels of Fortune'

11

major problems. The first of these was the question of the invalidity of Dunlop's patent of 1888 in the light of the existence of the earlier patent of Thomson, 43 years before. No stigma attaches to Dunlop in this matter. He knew nothing of Thomson's work. He started from scratch, with a pressing need to bring comfort to the bicycle rider. He produced a truly novel invention to meet the needs of 1888, with just as much genius in its devising as was shown by his fellow Scot, who had had so little luck with the same idea, nearly half a century earlier.

The Dunlop patent

The Patent Office of the day gave Dunlop no help. His patent was accepted in July 1888, the complete specification was deposited in November, dated October 31st and it was completed on December 7th. At the time of the founding of the Pneumatic Tyre and Booths Cycle Agency, Dunlop was asked about the soundness of his patents and is reported to have said that he considered them quite safe.

About the middle of 1890, a London patent agent saw a copy of a leaflet compiled in 1887, by William Ames, a Londoner, who was studying the problem of providing bicycles with improved insulation against vibration. The leaflet was a selected list of 'Elastic wheels', chosen from eighty specifications filed by the Patent Office between 1772 and 1887. Among the four chosen was Thomson's 1845 invention with its drawings. The patent agent passed the leaflet to a friend of Dunlop, and Dunlop in his turn showed it to the board of the new company, on 11 September 1890. By the end of that month the existence of the Thomson patent was 'published to the world at large' to use du Cros' words.

Thomson and Dunlop patents

The stature of the Thomson and Dunlop inventions may be judged by comparing the two patent specifications. Thomson presents an engineering specification for what he has invented and proceeds to work out its implications to the last detail and to see uses for the idea in fields outside that of the road vehicle. Dunlop's specification, on the other hand, is brief in the extreme. The original specification in its provisional form consisted of three lines of type, containing forty-four words. This covers the principle only and ends airily: ' . . . . . *to be attached to the wheel or wheels in such a method as may be found most suitable.*' The complete specification was longer, practically a whole page, and this was amended in July 1892, so that later editions made it plain that the claim was restricted to a very narrow field, that of a hollow tyre of rubber, surrounded by a casing of canvas, or other suitable material, protected by a tread and secured to the wheel by

12

a suitable cement or other means.

This limitation underlined the fact that the Dunlop patent had nothing patentable in it, in view of Thomson's earlier work. Patent offices in other countries, e.g. France, refused to accept the Dunlop application as valid.

In spite of these difficulties, which were a great embarrassment to his father's company, Sir Arthur du Cros wrote benevolently: *'There can be no monopoly of interest and therefore no end to unconscious plagiarism. Progress can be compared to a chain in which no one link is of greater importance than the other, and even though Dunlop's claim to the envied position of the first link must be ruled out, yet the chain of progress might never have been forged without him. The inventor, the adaptor, the improvers and all those who commercialised their ideas, were all links in the chain and it is invidious to deny honours to any in a sequence in which all are necessary to achieve the goal.'*

Far more important than mourning over the fact that the patent was invalid was the work which had to be done to make the invention more commercially usable. The major problem here was the crudity of the construction. The 'mummy' tyre was a fixture on the rim. Each time it suffered a puncture, the casing had to be soaked apart with naphtha, in order to reach the tube inside. After the necessary patch repair, the tube was replaced and the casing built up again with solution and the repaired part refixed on the wheel. This was a tiresome process and the user was not always capable of making a satisfactory repair himself.

The need for detachability

The first need was to work out a way in which the construction of the tyre and wheel could be modified, so that they became independent parts of the whole. This was to make it possible to sell complete tyres over the counter, which the customer could then take away and fit easily for himself to the wheels of his machine.

This was a second-order problem of invention. The engineer was shown the tyre as it existed and set the problem of separating it from the mummy-like binding on the rim. By 1890 this problem was occupying the minds of many men, none of whom would perhaps have invented the basic principle of the tyre, but who were nevertheless capable of tackling the practical problem of improving its construction and design.

The first and most successful answer came from a young engineer, of Tottenham, Middlesex, Charles Kingston Welch. He was the son

C. K. Welch, wired-on tyre

13

of the owner of a small engineering business and the originator of a number of patents covering improvements to bicycles. Welch, who was 29 at the time, began with the notion of putting wires into the edges of a horseshoe-shaped tyre and seating these inextensible edges on a rim with ledges or seats for them to locate upon. The first idea was a wire with its two ends joined by a screw-connector, which could be undone for fitting and then reconnected when the tyre was in position on the rim. This was soon discarded in favour of an endless circle of wire, together with a rim with a 'well' in the centre of its section (Figure 2·7). This was an elegant solution to the problem. The 'mummy' was replaced by a simple separate cover and tube, with no loose parts, and they were fitted to a similarly simple one-piece rim.

Du Cros, who tells the story of this invention with an eye-witness account by the inventor's brother, says that the experiments took only two or three days, before the elegant solution was found to the problem.

The process of fitting the wired-edge cover to the well-base rim consists of merely pushing part of the cover edge into the well of the rim, and then working the rest of the edge over the rim flange. This process is reversed, with the help of small levers, when the cover comes to be removed. The invention was patented on 16 September 1890. It was bought up immediately by the Pneumatic Tyre Company, who now, at last, had a valid patent on an extremely attractive form of tyre and were really in business.

Other people were, however, engaged on the problem of tyre removability. Thirty-six days after Welch's application for a patent there came another of practically equal merit. The inventor was an American, who was working in Scotland.

W. E. Bartlett, beaded-edge tyre

The North British Rubber Company had been established in Edinburgh, in 1855, by an American firm who wished to extend their manufacture of rubber galoshes to Great Britain. William Erskine Bartlett, born in Springfield, Massachusetts, a nephew of the managing director of the organisation, came to Scotland in 1870. He remained at Castle Mills, Edinburgh, eventually becoming managing director himself, and he died in 1900.

By 1890 Bartlett was a seasoned inventor, sixty years of age and the patentee of a cushion-type solid tyre, which was held in place on the wheel by turned-over edges on the rim. His solution to the problem of making the pneumatic tyre detachable used the same up-turned rim edge as had been employed to locate the cushion tyre. The tyre had no wires in its edges, but they contained a hardened, but still stretch-able rubber core. The design in the patent is shown in Figure 2·8. In this form it was found that the inflation pressure could stretch the deformable edge of the cover, until it came over the edge of the rim. The rim profile was therefore modified, so that the edges were in-turned like a hook, and the edge of the cover was similarly formed, to catch underneath the turned-over rim (Figure 2·9).

The Pneumatic Tyre Company realised that, in these two modifi-cations to the basic reinvention by Dunlop, lay the path forward to commercial success. The rights for Great Britain for the Welch patent were bought for £5000. Welch joined the company as technical advisor and the new wired-edge cycle tyres were marketed under the name Dunlop-Welch.

Dunlop-Welch

The English rights to the Bartlett patent were also acquired, for another £200,000, the inventor retaining the right to make tyres in Scotland, paying a royalty of 2/6d (12½p) per tyre to the Pneumatic Tyre Company.

There is a story of how far invention, directed towards the perfect-ing of the pneumatic tyre, proceeded inside the organisation of the Pneumatic Tyre Company itself. A racing cyclist, Thomas W. Robertson, of Belfast, was engaged to run the all-important repair department. This man had a very close view of the problem of non-detachability. He saw the messy business of soaking the tyres apart with naphtha, mending the punctures in the tubes, and then remaking the mummy casing on the wheel. He had the idea of a cover with wire in the edges, the ends of the wire being bent over, passed through holes in the rim, and secured with nuts on the outside. This was patented in the name of Robertson and the Company, in November 1890, ten weeks after the Welch patent, which rendered it invalid. One day before this Robertson patent came another by an indepen-dent inventor, Trigwell, also covering a tyre with wired edges.

A word about the fortunes of J. B. Dunlop himself in all this. He had received £300 in cash and three thousand one pound shares in the new company. His reaction to the discovery, that his patent on the pneumatic tyre was invalid, was to swing right away from the air tyre and to direct his work to the provision of added comfort in the cycle itself. He patented a bicycle in October 1889, with a frame made up completely of leaf-springs, and fitted with cushion solid tyres. This device, and Dunlop's faith in it, were soon swept away by the flowing tide of acceptance of the Welch and Bartlett detachable pneumatic tyres. From this point, Dunlop's personal part in the development of the pneumatic tyre and of the company began to decline, until finally, in March 1895, he severed his connection by resigning his directorship.

Dunlop's 'History'

At the end of his life, John Boyd Dunlop wrote a short account of the invention which will always be associated with his name. It had been hoped that his son Johnnie would have written this story, but unhappily he died two years before his father. This led the old man to work on some notes which he had already partly assembled. The result was a small book, 'The History of the Pneumatic Tyre', published in Dublin in 1924, three years after his death. His daughter, Mrs Jean McClintock, in a foreword, describes it as a 'first rough sketch, crude and unfinished.'

However, it is the story in the inventor's own words and is of great interest, even though it has to be remembered that we are reading the record, set down by an octogenarian, recollecting something in which he was involved forty years earlier, and not even trying to check the accuracy of his memory of dates or references.

CHAPTER 3

First Problems Solved

The development of a tyre valve, which was so satisfactory that it has continued in use until this day, is the next achievement to be chronicled. It should be noted first that a valve patented by J. B. Dunlop in March, 1889 was a step forward. It was designed as part of the tyre's engineering, and not just borrowed from a football as the original valve had been. But it had the great disadvantage that, once inflated, the tyre could not be deflated. The way in which the field of invention was open, in those days, to all who wished to take part, is well illustrated by the manner in which the problem was solved.

The inventor in question was Charles Woods, a cotton-spinner, whose brother was a director of the Pneumatic Tyre Company. The device is shown in (Figure 3·1). The valve is in two main parts, a cylindrical body, bolted into the tube, and an internal plug, the two being held together by a circular retaining collar. The plug is partially drilled through, axially, but has a blind inner end. In the side of the plug a hole is drilled through to meet the axial hole. The plug is then covered by a rubber sleeve, consisting of an inch-long length of thin, stretchable, fine-bore rubber tube. The outer end of this tube is pulled round an enlargement of the stem, and this rubber seals against a conical seating in the end of the valve body, when the retaining nut is tightened.

When air is pumped into the central stem, the rubber tube is distended, by air passing through the side passage, and this air is allowed to enter the inner tube of the tyre. There is no return through the valve, as the air inside the inner tube presses the valve rubber against

17

the plug and so seals the lateral hole in it. Deflation is carried out readily simply by unscrewing the retaining ring-nut and withdrawing the valve plug complete.

It will be noted that the plug has two wings on it, which locate in slots cut in the end of the valve body, and that the plug and the body have conical seatings, which as already mentioned, are sealed together by the outer end of the valve rubber. The valve is very simple and works well. The only expendable part is the rubber tubing of the valve, which perishes in time. Replacement is as cheap as it is simple.

This little component must rank as one of the pioneer inventions, which did much to help the pneumatic tyre on its progress into general use. It represents the successful solution of a problem, with a device of low cost and extreme simplicity. It is a foretaste of the modern science of value analysis, with an engineer forsaking the metal springs and other devices of his craft, which would be idle for practically the whole of their lives, and turning to a tiny piece of rubber tubing for the answer to his problem.

The Woods valve was patented in March 1891. The inventor asked for £1000 for his work, which was a large sum in those days. According to du Cros, the company, who were poor, offered him 3d. (1¼p) a valve, or a monopoly of its production, but Woods stuck to his terms and received the £1000.

Subsequent modifications to the valve have been confined to the manufacture of specially moulded or dipped rubbers, shaped to fit round the plug and replacing the short lengths of straight rubber tube. These are details only, the original idea remaining unmodified and in use worldwide.

Many inventions

The years which followed, through the early 'nineties, and up to the turn of the century, were years of prolific invention in the field of the pneumatic tyre. A paper by W. H. Paull, in March 1891, gives a blow-by-blow account of this era of development. One is struck by the enormous activity and by the way in which, from about 1889 onwards, multitudes of inventors were turning over the same problems, and producing answers which were often in similar terms.

It would be tedious to list in great detail what was done, but it is profitable to say something about the main problems which were tackled, and to name some of the inventors whose work was to endure as part of the development progress of the tyre.

Puncture resistance

Punctures were the first difficulty encountered by users of the new

18

tyre. A cycle cover is a relatively thin structure. The rubber used in those days was a pure natural rubber-gum, with no great resistance to cutting or penetration. Roads and other surfaces were crude and not well maintained. Penetrations of tyres by thorns, flint flakes, boot nails and similar objects were common, and the repair of the damage was not very reliable.

Of the inventors who tackled this and other tyre problems, it may be said that they came from all walks of life. The main common factor was that they were mostly young and enthusiastic for the new tyre. It has been said that, in the absence of such modern time-fillers as television and the football pools, invention was a national pastime.

There were several lines of attack on the puncture problem. People inside the industry tended to think in terms of the properties of rubber, and to devise materials to meet the need. C. H. Gray, of the Silvertown Rubber Company produced a single-tube tyre, with an inner lining of plastic uncured rubber. This automatically flowed into any punctures and filled them up, sealing them from the inside. This idea worked, as most of them did at first, but the lining soon hardened and perished and became ineffective.

Several inventors tackled the problem from the same position in the tyre, but using different techniques. They provided the self-sealing inner lining in the form of a layer of rubber under compression, which when pierced by a puncturing object, sealed itself up by its own internal compression. Such layers were often achieved by carrying out the first stages of cover building inside-out, applying the inner-lining rubber to the outer surface of the casing and then turning it, so that the longer length of lining became compressed when reduced to the shorter inner circumference. Thus, it tended to close up both on puncturing objects and on the holes left on their withdrawal from the tyre.

Self-sealing tyres

Other ideas about puncture prevention came from those with no knowledge of rubber techniques. The suggestion most frequently proposed was based on putting a layer of impenetrable material between the tread and the casing of the tyre, to deflect nails and other puncture producing objects. The favourite material was a strip of steel, such as in a clock spring or a steel tape. The suggestion, although excellent as a puncture repellent, was not satisfactory as a component of a tyre casing. Steel is incapable of the type of deformation which takes place in the contact area of a tyre on the ground,

Armour plating

19

where simultaneous shortening of length and decrease in width occur. It was difficult to stick the parts of such a composite steel and fabric tyre together, and once assembled the metal component was incompatible with the rest of the casing and fought continuously to get out, as the tyre ran.

W. H. Paull, writing of conditions at the end of the last century, comments on the way in which the same ideas were repeated, over and over again, in tyre patents. *"As an instance"*, he says, *"may be mentioned the idea of enclosing a metal band within the tread of a tyre, for puncture resisting purposes. This, although proved to be practically useless, has been the subject of some six hundred patents, and is still being patented."*

A 'tubeless' tyre

1892 saw a patent by Smallman, which was commercially promoted as the Fleuss tubeless tyre. This is shown in (Figure 3·2). The design had a flexible rubber extension to one edge of the cover and this was arranged to seal over the other edge under the effect of the inflation pressure, so that the tyre was airtight without any tube. The construction overcame the problem of fitting a tubeless tyre to a wire-spoked cycle wheel, since the overlapping extensions at the edge of the cover lay across the holes in the rim, in which the spoke-heads seated, which could never be made airtight. The tyre was made by Capon Heaton, at Hazelwell Mills, Stirchley, Birmingham. Among the claims made for it was that it could readily be mended, after puncture, by sticking adhesive stamp-paper over the holes in the smooth inner lining.

W. H. Paull, looks back over the first twelve years since Dunlop's reinvention, and says prophetically: "... *I look to some form of tubeless tyre as one of the tyres of the future.*"

In January 1893 a major improvement was made in the strength of the rims on which the early cycle tyres were mounted. This was the work of Frederick Westwood, of Birmingham. The original Welch well-base rim was weak as a structure and, in the frequent minor bumps and impacts suffered by the users of the pneumatic tyre, rims often became distorted, both laterally and radially.

The Westwood Rim

The Westwood invention contributed a major increase in strength by relatively simple means. The steel strip, from which the rim was rolled, was made wider and its edges were turned over and brazed to the surface of the tyre seats (Figure 3·3). This provided the rim with tubular edges and gave it a great increase in rigidity and strength. This

20

simple fundamental patent was also acquired by the Pneumatic Tyre Company. Westwood's rim is still in use today. It was one of the first of a class of improvements to pneumatic tyre equipment, where an increase in cost is accompanied by an improvement in performance of such a magnitude that the new product becomes quickly established, and renders the earlier cheaper construction obsolete.

During these early years, the fabric of which the tyre casing was built also came in for scrutiny. As with so many inventions, it was deficiencies in the functioning of tyres made with makeshift fabrics, that led to the recognition of the desirable features, and to the design of more suitable materials, having accurately defined properties. **Tyre fabrics**

The original Dunlop tyre was built of a cloth known as Gent's yacht sailcloth. This was a fine canvas type of material, cross-woven, with equal strength and thickness of the threads in the two directions, warp and weft. The development of the new tyre, as it came into early commercial production, continued to be based on the use of cross-woven fabrics of this kind (Figure 3.4).

In use in tyres, these canvasses did not give completely satisfactory service. During the flexing of the tyre on the road, as it revolved under load, the threads of the two components of the cross-woven fabrics sawed upon each other until, sooner or later, they cut through each other, so that the tyre casing broke up. The next significant group of inventions was directed to improving this casing deficiency. **Casing fatigue**

All users of pneumatic tyres became aware of this problem of casing fatigue. The deficiencies of cross-woven fabrics were exposed for all to see, and as a challenge to be met by the discovery of something better. It is not surprising that the same kind of answer was arrived at by several inventors, at about the same time.

The logical approach to the problem was along these lines: The casing of the tyres failed because the threads of warp and weft sawed on one another as the tyre revolved. Therefore if the cross-over points between the threads, which form what are graphically described as 'knuckles' in the textile trade, could be eliminated, then the chafing in the fabric might be practically eliminated.

From these conclusions it was a short step to the production of a fabric construction, in which the cross-woven layout was abandoned and in which the two kinds of threads, which make up the material, were no longer woven, but were kept in two distinct layers, separated by a film of rubber. In the tyre, built from such a 'fabric', this elimin- **Cord constructions**

21

ated the 'knuckles' and the chafing, and led both to an improvement in casing life and a detectable reduction in the effort required to pedal the cycle (Figure 3·5).

J. F. Palmer

Now as to dates. The name which everyone remembers is that of John Fullerton Palmer, whose patents on 'all warp' fabric were filed in America in the autumn of 1892 and in England some six months later. This patent was a strong one and companies were set up, to exploit the new process, in the United Kingdom and elsewhere.

David Moseley

There were many other inventors working on this problem of the properties required in a tyre casing. So far as the Pneumatic Tyre Company was concerned, the important name was that of David Moseley, of Manchester, who had a patent, dated as early as 1888, on a weftless fabric known as Flexifort. This patent was upheld in the English courts and, so far as this country was concerned, the Palmer patents were invalid.

Weftless cord

The Pneumatic Tyre Company were also involved directly in these developments. Among the collection at the Science Museum, at South Kensington, there is a sample, dated 1892, of a weftless silk fabric, made by J. B. Dunlop, for use in experimental tyres. C. K. Welch, of the company, took the cord principle to its engineering limit, in patents dated 1894-95, which arranged the cord of the weftless plies so that they were tangential to the rim-edge, and capable of the most effective transmission of drive and braking from wheel to road.

Many other inventors worked in this field and were spurred on by the demands which were apparent for a material for tyre casings, which was more suitable than the makeshift canvasses which were in use. Many of these were responsible for patents which were never exploited. Some were in that most embarrassing class of inventors, who have an idea, but who lack the engineering or technical skill to be able to explain what it is that they are doing, or how it is supposed to work. It is an odd reflection, that half a century later, in the 'fifties and 'sixties, when the latest patents on advanced methods of tyre construction were being scrutinised, many of these old patents, from the earliest years of the cycle tyre, were often produced as devastating evidence of what is termed 'prior use' of ideas which the modern inventors were claiming as brand new.

It will be recognized that, although the weftless cord casing gave a large improvement in casing performance, it did create some problems of its own. The ideal method of production of true weftless material is to start with what is called a creel of bobbins of cord, such as would be used to feed the warp thread into a loom. The assembled threads are then passed into a calender nip, where they are coated with films of rubber, top and bottom. In this way a managable rubbered sheet is produced, which can be treated as if it were a woven fabric. In the absence of a creel, it is possible to wind the warp threads side by side on a roller or 'beam', and then to draw them off again into the calender for rubbering. While on the beam the material is storable and transportable.

It was to overcome this difficulty of handling a formless raw fabric that a minor retreat was made from the completely weftless concept. This was done by reducing the weft component of the material to a skeleton of thin 'pick' threads, of the gauge of thin sewing cotton, spaced out about half an inch or so apart in the warp threads. This type of 'woven cord' has practically the same advantage in fatigue resistance as has a completely weftless structure. From the practical production angle, it presents the cord suppliers and the tyre factory with a material which can be handled very readily in the plants (Figure 3·6).

Woven cord

CHAPTER 4

The Cycle Tyre Completed

By the middle of the 'nineties the cycle tyre had reached the end of its major development. Very little has needed to be done to it since.

Road grip

The final feature to receive attention was the provision of adequate grip on the road, although the problem was as much one of road conditions as of the properties of the tyre itself. The new-fangled tyre, in spite of its greatly improved comfort and cushioning, did not grip the road very well. Like the small-section solid or cushion tyres which it superseded, it had a smooth-surfaced tread.

The roads of the day had a loose surface, strewn with sand, smooth gravel or other stone. (At worst this was almost as bad as trying to run on a tray of small ball-bearings.) Under conditions where the road consisted of a layer of fine sand spread over a hard base the danger of the tyre losing its grip and slipping sideways was always present, even in dry conditions. Furthermore, the bigger contact area and lower contact pressure of the pneumatic tyre on the road made it more liable to skid, than the small section solid tyre. The latter, with high contact pressure over a very small area of contact, was better able to dig into loose surfaces and to obtain a grip which depended on a deep mechanical lock, rather than on surface friction.

It must be understood that the tarmac road had not been invented and the only Macadam roads in existence were those with waterbound stones rolled into the surface. Much of the road system in cities was of granite setts, with polished surfaces and a network of sunken joints between.

The first tyre moulds

It was to improve tyre grip on roads, such as these, that tread patterns were added to tyres. The move was at first part of a general

24

Figure 3.1
The Wood cycle valve, 1891. The valve mechanism consists of a brass plug 'D', drilled lengthwise and with an orifice as shown in the side, near the blind end. This plug is covered with a short length of rubber tubing, shown stretched and separated at 'C'. The plug is held in the valve stem by the collar 'E', the joint being sealed by the expanded lower end of the rubber. On inflation through the stem, air enters the tyre through the lateral hole in the plug, escaping between the rubber tube and the plug, but it cannot return, as the internal pressure holds the rubber tube against the surface of the plug and seals the hole.

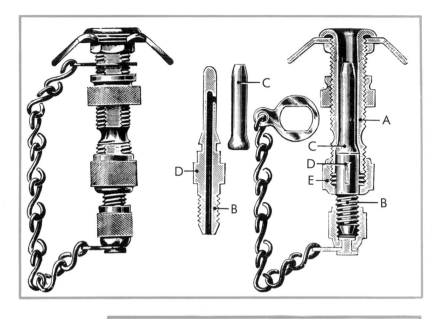

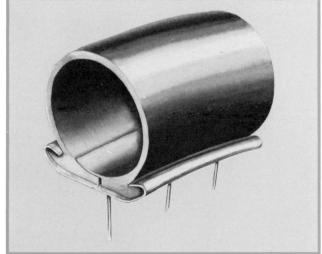

Figure 3.2
The Fleuss tubeless cycle tyre, 1892. A tubeless construction with a rubber lined casing, having extensions to the cover edges, which overlap, covering the spoke-heads in the rim and sealing together under the internal pressure.

Figure 3.3
The Westwood cycle rim, 1893. The rim is greatly strengthened by rolling the edges over and brazing circumferentially to form tubular sections.

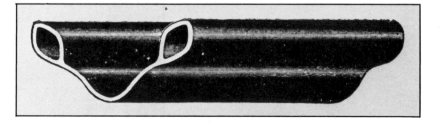

Figure 3.4.
Woven canvas, with warp and weft threads crossing to form 'knuckles' which produce sawing of cord on cord during flexing in a tyre.

Figure 3.5.
Weftless cord fabric, used in tyre building, so that the threads in the two directions are separated by a layer of rubber compound. The 'knuckles' are removed and internal chafing in the fabric is prevented. Less effort is also required to roll the tyre along the road.

Figure 3.6.
'Woven' cord fabric, with the weft threads replaced by a skeleton of thin 'pick' threads, enabling the practically weftless material to be handled as a sheet in the factory.

Figure 4.1
The iron ring on which cycle tyres were assembled. The strip of tread and sidewall rubber was applied first and received its pattern from the engraving round the centre of the ring. The canvas or cord casing was then added, enclosing wire or hard rubber edges or beads. The tyre was then wrapped onto the ring with a cloth bandage and vulcanised in open steam. Afterwards the tyre was stripped from the ring and turned inside out.

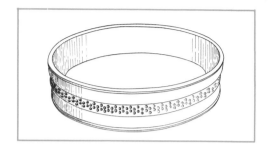

Figure 4.2
The Doughty press for moulding cycle tyres. The diagrams, from the Patent Specifications, show how the two halves of the mould are carried in steam-heated chests forming the top and bottom platens of the press. The uncured tyre is fitted over the 'head' which is shown between the platens and as the press closes the 'head' expands, as shown in the plan views to form a complete circle and to force the tyre into contact with the mould.

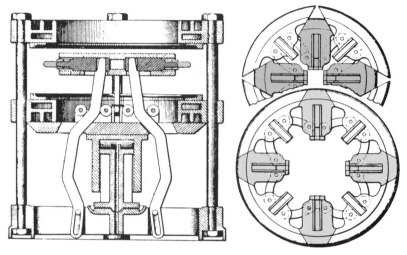

Figure 4.3
Doughty presses in the cycle tyre shop at Aston. The presses are seen open, as in the patent drawing. Note the lagged steam chests above and below the opening of the press.

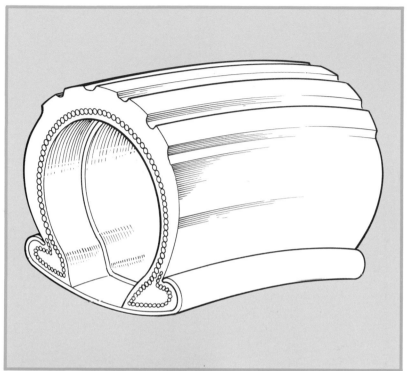

Figure 4.4.
Ribbed cycle tyre with plenty of circumferential edges to guard against sideways skidding.

The self-advertising tyre.

Figure 4.5.
Dunlop Welch wired type of tyre for horse-drawn carriages. Dunlop's cycle tyre adapted to cover the field of Thomson's original invention.

tidying up of the outside of the cycle cover. This was achieved by vulcanising it in contact with some kind of a mould. Moulding gave the outside of the tyre a smooth finish, it enabled names and sizes, engraved in the mould surface, to appear as sharp, clear, raised lettering on the tyre wall, and it made it possible for instructions, such as 'Inflate Hard' to be included.

Some of the earliest of these moulded tyres were made by a flat-building operation, in which the tyre was assembled, inside out, on the outside of a circular iron ring (Figure 4·1). The surface of the ring had the pattern and engraving cut into it and the tyre was assembled from the outside inwards. The strip of extruded tread and sidewall rubber was laid down first and then the plies and the coils of bead-wire or rubber bead cores added.

The completed tyre was bound tightly against the surface of the drum, by a wrapping of canvas bandage. A number of these drums, bearing their built-up tyre casings, were then heated in open steam in an autoclave or 'pan' fed with the steam under pressure. After the moulding process, the tyres were stripped from their iron rings and turned inside out, so that the patterned surface became the outer surface of the cover. The final shaping of the tyre into its correct toroidal tyre form was carried out by the user in the process of the first inflation.

The next step was the development of a simple enclosed moulding plant to replace the treatment in open steam. The most famous is that associated with the name of H. J. Doughty, which was introduced in 1896. Here the mould was made in full toroidal form and was divided into three parts (Figure 4·2). The tread pattern was engraved in the inner surface of a ring, which extended just below the edge of the road-contacting surface of the tread. The mould was completed by two side pieces which covered the sidewall areas of the tyre and included the lettering and size-marking.

These three parts of the tyre mould were mounted in a steam-heated press, so that heat could be fed into the unvulcanised tyre, through all the surfaces of the mould, and so cause the necessary combination of the rubber and sulphur, in the mixed compounds used in tread and casing. The two walls received their heat direct from the steam-heated platens of the press, to which they were bolted. The tread ring was fed with heat from its own steam-heated annulus with which it was surrounded.

The Doughty press

25

The Doughty 'head'

The most ingenious part of the Doughty press was the mechanical means used for supporting the tyre from the inside and applying a thrust to cause it to fill the mould and thus receive its impress. It would have been possible to do this by the use of an air tube of some kind, as was subsequently done in the manufacture of larger tyres. Doughty, as an engineer, ignored such contraptions, and worked out the details of a solid internal core and a method of cutting it into six or eight segments and arranging their travel radially into the mould, so that when 'home' they were locked into a continuous solid ring. This was good engineering, capable of achievement and maintenance under the conditions found in the workshops of the day. The Doughty head and its surrounding press mould became the standard method of moulding the European cycle tyre, for more than half a century (Figure 4·3).

The Doughty head leaves its signature on the inner surface of the cover, in the form of a series of horseshoe-shaped imprints running from bead to bead at the segment joints. The cycle tyre manufacturer looks critically at these impressions, as their prominence or irregularity is the first sign that the Doughty head is becoming worn or out of adjustment.

The Doughty press was an American invention. The licence for its use in the United Kingdom was obtained by the Byrne Brothers India Rubber Company Limited, an English Company founded by the Byrne brothers in 1896. In 1898 the shares of that Company were acquired from the brothers by The Dunlop Pneumatic Tyre Company Limited. To fill in the gaps it should be noted that sequence of Company names went as follows: in 1894 The Pneumatic Tyre and Booths Cycle Agency Limited changed its name to The Pneumatic Tyre Company Limited; in 1896 the name changed again to The Dunlop Pneumatic Tyre Company Limited, finally in 1900 the combined Dunlop and Byrne companies became The Dunlop Rubber Company Limited. A year later, 1901, manufacture was concentrated in Birmingham in the factories at Aston Cross and at Manor Mills.

Tread patterns

It was now possible for cycle tyres to have tread patterns, since they were fully-moulded articles. The pattern was produced by turning, milling and engraving the iron or steel tread rim of the Doughty mould. The earliest designs were plain circumferential ribs. This suited the mould maker, as he could produce such a pattern by a simple turning operation. It also suited the salesman and his customer,

26

since the main objective was to secure protection against lateral skidding, or the falling-down, of the bicycle, and a pattern with plenty of lateral edges had obvious advantages (Figure 4·4).

However, it was not long before the publicity man took a hand in the design of tyre treads, and tyres came on to the market with the maker's name as the central feature of the tread. In 1891 the cyclist had the joy of leaving a trail of DUNLOP DUNLOP DUNLOP along the road, in the soft mud on wet days and in the dust on dry ones. As the framework round this lettering still consisted of a system of circumferential ribs, the resistance of the tyre to sideslip was not measurably affected. And so an era of fancy tread patterns started.

Nothing more need be said, at this stage, about tread pattern design, but it is doubtful if, even today, we can make much contribution by tread pattern modification to the performance of cycle tyres for general use. In the field of cycle racing the requirements were closely defined from the start, and a system of fine ribs for lateral grip combined with file pattern bands for tractive grip, was introduced for track and path racing and is still in use.

By the end of the last half of the 'nineties, the cycle tyre was perfected. It had a casing of weftless (or virtually weftless) cotton, it had a functional and commercially acceptable tread pattern, and it was an extremely cheap and highly efficient component of the bicycle.

Early in the era of the bicycle tyre, the Pneumatic Tyre Company revived interest in the new tyre for horse-drawn carriages. The Dunlop-Welch wired tyre was eminently suitable for the purpose, and the combination of large overall diameter and relatively small section made it possible to apply the methods of manufacture which had been worked out for cycle tyres.

Carriage tyres again

Du Cros records how, in 1892, a dogcart was bought by the Company for experimental purposes, and that this appeared on the streets of Coventry, behind a prizewinner from the Dublin horseshow, and that the perfectly silent pneumatic wheels became the talk of the town.

Typical examples of these, in the Dunlop collection, are between 40″ and 50″ in diameter (Figure 4·5).

In 1894, du Cros read a paper to the British Coachbuilders' Association, on pneumatic tyres for carriages. He records that it had little or no effect on the somnolence of that august body.

In preparation for the paper some test results were prepared, comparing the new tyres with steel rims. These are quoted in 'Wheels of Fortune', on the same page as the Thomson results. The two sets of figures lead the reader to realise that du Cros had merely brought Thomson's experimental data up to date by minor adjustments.

The pneumatic carriage tyre did, however, have a limited application.

For a sidelight on the social status which a carriage so equipped brought, the reader should see the account of the gummiradler, in the chapter 'Caprice Viennoise' of Vicki Baum's book about the rubber industry, "The Weeping Wood" (1945).

As the horse-drawn carriage gave way to the motor car the importance of this type of tyre declined, but the pneumatic tyre is still used on special vehicles, such as the trotting frame, and there is an overlap between the disappearance of the tyre from the road on gentlemen's carriages, and the reappearance of it as the new equipment for farm carts and trailers, in the 'thirties.

CHAPTER 5

Pneumatic Tyres & the Motor Car

While Dunlop's pneumatic tyre was being developed, to meet the needs of the energetic young men of the cycle age, their elder and more affluent brothers were working on the basic idea of a self-propelling road vehicle, the automobile.

This is no place to review the very earliest stages of the invention of such vehicles, which go back to William Murdock and Nicholas Cugnot, in the seventeen-sixties; to Trevethick at the turn of the nineteenth century; and to such mighty vehicles as the steel shod steam coaches of Griffiths and Church, Scott Russell and Gurney, in the first quarter of the new century. Church's coach carried fifty people, 28 inside and the rest on top.

By 1890, the heavy steam engine was no longer the only available source of power. The arrival of the smaller, lighter petrol engine had led to work by Marcus, in 1885, and by the partnership of Daimler and Benz, which brought the possibility of a horseless carriage for family or personal use into being.

Although the key developments took place in Germany, there was considerable activity in France. Here de Dion with Bouton, Peugeot and the Panhard-Levassor partnership carried out significant development work.

Automobile prehistory

In order to realise the advantages which were to be obtained, by applying the pneumatic tyre to these early cars, we should look for a while at the examples illustrated. The earliest of all were veritable 'horseless carriages'. In the Canstatt-Daimler (Figure 5·1), for example, the horse has obviously only just left, and the studs by which his harness was formerly attached are still left in place. These studs were, in fact, often brought back into service, when after one of the frequent engine failures, the horse was recalled, to rescue the car and to bring it ignominiously home.

These vehicles either had solid rubber tyres of small section or were still on steel rims.

Some pioneer cars

By 1895 automobile design had become more sophisticated and light vehicles, designed afresh to be self-powered, were in use (Figure 5·2). These were mainly developed in France, where there were soon two-hundred different vehicle-building firms, compared with twenty-nine in Britain and only four in America.

The need for the pneumatic

The handling of the light cars, with their very direct steering, was harsh, especially on the rough road surfaces. Apart from control difficulties, speeds above 12 m.p.h. led to such vibration that the vehicle rapidly shook itself to pieces. There was obvious opportunity here for the pneumatic tyre.

The pioneers in the application of the pneumatic tyre to the car were the Michelin brothers, Andre and Edouard, who were already well-established in the cycle tyre field. A long-distance race from Paris to Brest and back to Paris, in 1891, had already proved a triumph. Their rider, in spite of five punctures in the 750 mile race, finished eight hours ahead of the second man.

Michelin Paris-Bordeaux 1895

The brothers announced that they would have pneumatic tyres ready for use on cars, by the time of the 745-mile Paris-Bordeaux race in 1895. No car manufacturer was willing to submit his vehicle to such a dangerous experiment, or to add the uncertainties of the pneumatic tyre to the others which beset him at every point of design. The brothers therefore bought a 4 horse-power Daimler engine and built their own car to run on the first pneumatic tyres ever designed for a car (Figure 5·3).

Their car did not win the race. Due to some confusion it did not actually figure among the starters in the official list. But the brothers did complete the course and were among the nine vehicles still running at the finish. All that we learn of tyre performance is that the entire stock of 24 spare tubes was used up in the course of the race. The winner's speed was 15 m.p.h.

Over the next ten years, there was great activity in the development of pneumatic tyres for motor vehicles. Much of this took place in France, but parallel development of a British automobile industry proceded rapidly.

30

It is surprising that, in developing tyres for early motor cars, the lessons which had been so well-learned and the techniques which had been developed, in the field of cycle tyres, were completely ignored and disregarded. Thus, in 1896 the bicycle had cord tyres with anti-skid tread designs, moulded on their treads. Alongside it the early car had obsolete canvas casings in its tyres, which had no non-skid pattern whatsoever upon them.

Back to first base

This odd situation is some indication of the gulf which existed between the workers in the two fields. It may be added that the car casing stayed on woven fabric for another twenty-five years, while tread patterns caught up rather more quickly in only a decade.

The first few years of pneumatic tyres for cars have little interest from the technical standpoint. In order to understand what happened it is necessary to bear in mind the patent background which had been built up in terms of the cycle tyre and which was now to exert its hampering influence on the progress of automobile design.

In England the Pneumatic Tyre Company held the two main patents; those of Welch, covering the wired type and of Bartlett for the beaded-edge principle. The only pocket of privilege was in Scotland; Bartlett had a personal licence to manufacture his beaded-edge tyre through his connections with the North British Rubber Company.

Patent strangle-hold

Outside the United Kingdom, the Pneumatic Tyre Company's patent cover varied considerably. In France and Germany, where the development of the automobile was rapid, the wired type patent was strongly held, but Bartlett's beaded construction had not been so well covered by the Company and this construction was open for exploitation. It was this design that Michelin were able to use as the basic design for the first automobile tyre in the world.

In the U.S.A. the Pneumatic Tyre Company held strong Welch and Bartlett patents.

In Scotland, Mr Bartlett came to an arrangement with Michelin in France, to make beaded-edge car tyres for him. This arrangement was challenged by the Pneumatic Tyre Company but they lost their case and the appeal against the first judgement.

So it was that the French motor industry found itself using, as the standard tyre, a beaded-edge construction. Vehicles with these tyres were safe from prosecution for infringing the patents of the Pneumatic Tyre company provided they stayed in France, or came only temporarily into England on French cars. When such vehicles required tyre replacements in the United Kingdom then the Pneumatic Tyre company could, and did, exert a complete ban on the importation of French tyres which contravened their patents. This meant a conversion of the car to tyres made in England and led to a great deal of dissent among early motorists, who merely wished to buy as replacements the type of tyres which they had already been using.

So there came a few years of court wrangling about patent rights and about the legality of tyres made by various companies and in different places. Du Cros tells the story in detail and indicates what was commercially won by it. He gives us glimpses of the profit and loss account on these patent holdings, as for example:

> *paid to W. E. Bartlett* £200,000
> *received as royalties on Bartlett and*
> *Palmer tyres and for Clipper activities* £400,000

Finally, in 1904, the Welch patents expired and the Dunlop Rubber Company, held a celebration dinner, at which the Welch and Bartlett patents were ceremonially burnt. This action was widely acclaimed by many people who had never realised what the patent actions had been about and who had generally been irritated by the Company's efforts to maintain and defend its rights.

From the purely technical standpoint the effect of the imposition of the stranglehold on car tyre development, which the patent situation had exerted, resulted in the development of a less satisfactory tyre. The wired-type design was, and is, far safer. The beaded-edge tyre, although practicable in the small sections used on bicycles, runs into difficulties when scaled up to the larger sections needed for a heavy automobile. The increased area of cover hanging on the interlock of flexible bead and rim-edge turnover, made it necessary to use additional means of attachment of the beaded-edge tyre to the rim. This led to the use of security-bolts as a normal fitment (Figure 5·4). These were applied, as wedge-like locking devices, holding the bead into the rim, spaced out at intervals round the rim. The complication of fitting, which such additions make is best left to the imagination!

The patent restrictions also led to the use of various types of inferior tyre-to-rim attachments, simply because they evaded the terms of the patent. Only on such grounds can we excuse the complexity of such designs as the Collier tyre, of 1902 (Figure 5·5).

Figure 5.1, above
The Gottlieb Daimler, 1886. An obvious horseless carriage, with the horse only recently departed. Details at the front of the vehicle show where the shafts have been removed. and where they could be readily replaced if it had to be towed away.

Figure 5.2, below.
Daimler-Benz, 1894. A vehicle still showing some traces of horsedrawn origin, but designed to carry the driver in the centre of the wheelbase.

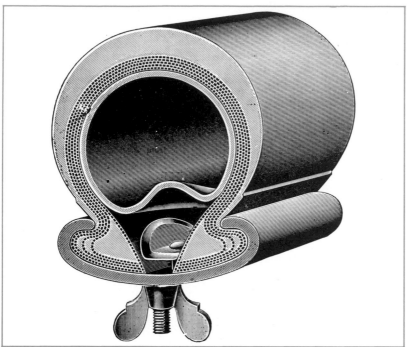

Figure 5.4.
Beaded edge car tyre, with smooth tread, with stretchable beads held in the turned-over edges of the rim, by security-bolts at intervals.

Figure 5.5, below left.
The Collier tyre, of 1902, designed to avoid the Welch wired-type patent. The steel bead-wires are replaced by springs, onto the coils of which are threaded retaining bolts, which are moulded into the tyre structure. These bolts pass through slots in the base of the rim and are retained by tubular threaded collars.

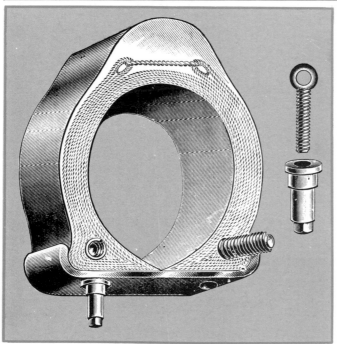

Figure 5.3, above.
The 4 horse-power Daimler engined car, built by the Michelin Brothers, and run in the 1895 Paris-Bordeaux race. In spite of many punctures the car was still running at the finish.

Figure 6.1A Top Right.
Dunlop wired-type car tyre, 1900,
on wellbase wheel. Multiple plies
of canvas with a single-strand wire
in the bead.

Figure 6.1B Centre.
Beaded-edge car tyre of the same
period, with extensible beads held
in the turn-over of the Bartlett rim.
(as mentioned in the text security
bolts were usually fitted to hold the
beads in the rim.)

Figure 6.2 Below.
The Parsons' Chain. To give increased grip in ice, snow or mud.
Shown fitted to an early type of tyre
with a narrow tread. The device
was popular for many years and
gave a marked increase in grip. It
was liable to tyre damage if used
over long periods.

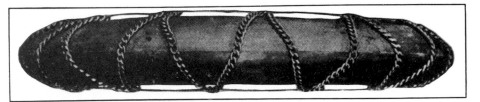

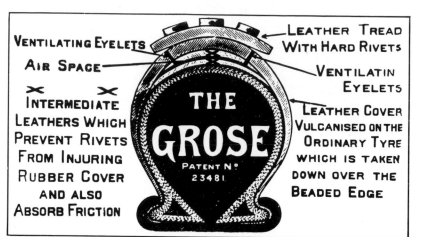

VENTILATING EYELETS

AIR SPACE

✕ ✕
INTERMEDIATE
LEATHERS WHICH
PREVENT RIVETS
FROM INJURING
RUBBER COVER
AND ALSO
ABSORB FRICTION

THE
GROSE
PATENT Nº
23481

LEATHER TREAD
WITH HARD RIVETS

VENTILATIN
EYELETS

LEATHER COVER
VULCANISED ON THE
ORDINARY TYRE
WHICH IS TAKEN
DOWN OVER THE
BEADED EDGE

Figure 6·3A.
The advertisement for the Grose non-skid band shows the complications involved in adding a leather tread, with steel studs, to an existing canvas tyre.

The device consists of a complete covering of leather, vulcanised onto the outer surface of the smooth-treaded tyre, and carried down into the turned-over edges of the rim.

Extra layers of leather are added to prevent chafing of the tyre by the bases of the steel studs. Provision is made for ventilation of the base of the leather bands, which suggests that overheating of the very thick composite tyre had already been encountered.

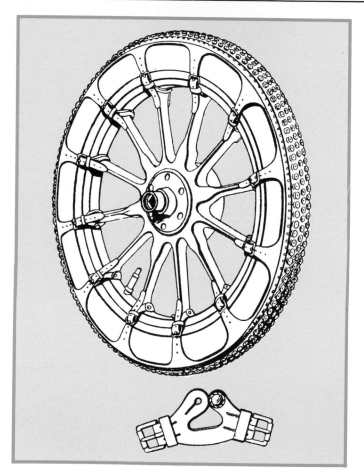

Figure 6·3B.
The Belgian Perfecter non-skid band consisted of a leather jacket with leather studs rivetted into its tread surface. The band covered only the tread and shoulders of the tyre and was held in place by straps extending down the sidewalls, which were fastened into buckles at each spoke of the wheel. At the foot of the drawing one of the double buckle devices is shown, with the button and eyelet arrangement for fixing it round the spoke.

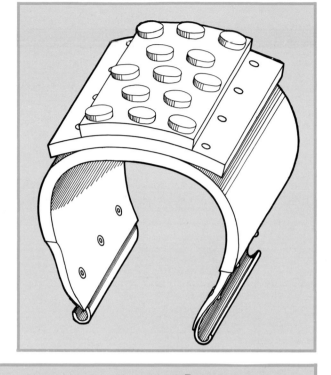

Figure 6·4A
The Brooklands non-skid band, again made of leather and fitting over the outer surface of a beaded-edge tyre. The device was not stuck to the tyre but was held in place by a system of spring-steel hooks, rivetted to the edges of the leather band and engaged with the turned-over edges of the rim.

The tread area of the band is reinforced by two extra strips of leather, the outer one carrying the studs, the inner ends of which are cushioned by the second leather band. The construction shown was liable to considerable chafing at the open edges of the inner leather tread band.

Figure 6·4B
French non-skid band designed to cover the tread portion only of the tyre. It is held in position by two wire cables running round the edges and fitting into buffed-out recesses in the shoulders of the tyre. A large groove buffed into the centre of the tread grips a keystone-shaped extension of the band, which encloses a compressed tubular rubber filling.

The steel studs are fixed in the outer of the two layers which make up the non-skid band.

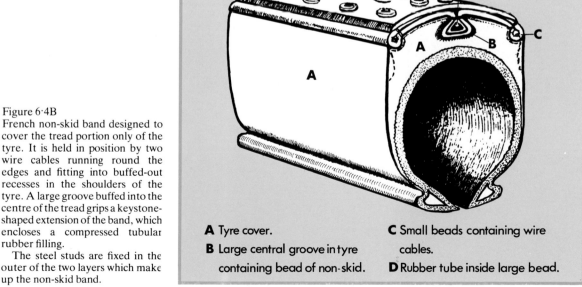

A Tyre cover.

B Large central groove in tyre containing bead of non-skid.

C Small beads containing wire cables.

D Rubber tube inside large bead.

Figure 6.5
Tyre with leather tread-band with inset steel studs.

Figure 6.6
Tyre with simple studded pattern produced from a mould in which a series of drilled recesses have been linked by circumferential slots.

Figure 6.7A Above.
The non-slipping tyre fitted to a car
of the period.

Figure 6.7B Top Right.
The first advertisement in the world
of a tyre with a non-slipping or non-
skid tread pattern. 1906.

Figure 6.8
Close-up of the tread of the Dunlop
non-slipping tread, showing the
impressions made by the metal
slugs pressed into the uncured
tread. The marks of the cloth bandage which held the slugs in position
during a cure in open steam can
also be seen on the surface of the
tread.

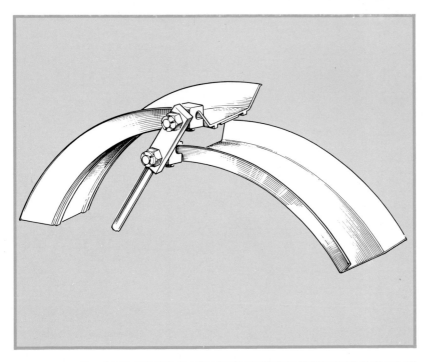

Figure 6.9,
A well-engineered split-rim, showing the lever device used to draw
one end of the rim inwards, so that
its circumference is reduced so that
the tyre may be fitted and removed.

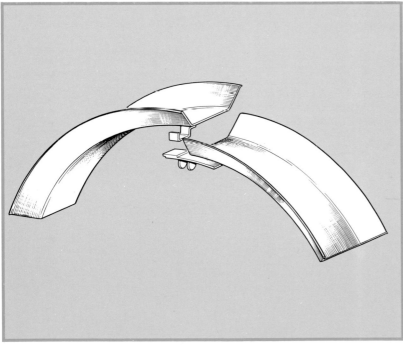

Figure 6·10.
Cheap form of split rim, used on
American trucks in the 'Twenties'.
with the two ends held together by
a simple turn-buckle lock.

Here the Welch patent is sidestepped, by substituting an annular spiral spring for the solid bunch of beadwires. Threaded onto this spring, at intervals, were retaining bolts moulded into the tyre structure. These extended radially inwards through the fabric of the tyre bead, and passed through slots in the base of the wheel rim, where they were secured by the addition of tubular, threaded collars at the rim base.

The process of fitting such a tyre must have been a tiresome and lengthy operation. It involved distortion of the bead when stretching it over the edge of the rim, followed by lining up all the retaining bolts with corresponding holes in the base of the rim, very limited adjustment being allowed by slots in the rim.

The acceptance of the pneumatic tyre, as an equipment for cars, was tentative. It took many years of slow improvement of the device, and of the way in which it was made, before it finally replaced the solid tyre. The following sequence of comments, from the 'correspondence' and 'news' columns of journals of the day, will illustrate the way in which progress was made, by a slow but steady overcoming of difficulties:

Motorists reactions

March 1900	A Daimler car made the journey from Coventry to London, 90 miles, in 4 hours 50 minutes, non-stop, on solid tyres. '*The newest French car would need the assistance of pneumatic tyres to equal this.*'
April 1900	Star cars; prices from 155 guineas on cushion tyres. Pneumatics 5 guineas extra.
May 1900	Basil Joy and Charles Rush, lecturing to the Institute of Junior Engineers: '*Pneumatic tyres, in some shape, are an almost absolute necessity for motor cars, both for comfort and for speed and also saving the motor from vibration. They are well worth the trouble entailed by punctures, to which they are very liable.*'
July 1900	A motor engineer in Paris finds that, on light cars, pneumatics wear out in 7,000 Kms. while solid tyres last 15,000 Kms.
September 1900	A correspondent writes: '*Pneumatics are desirable but not necessary. There is not a great deal of difference between the running of a Mors car on the pneumatic and solid tyres.*'

33

December 1901	Report of a Daimler 24 h.p. car, capable of 45 m.p.h., equipped with solids on the rear wheels and pneumatics on the fronts.
February 1902	*'The King's cars are on solid tyres and what is good enough for him is good enough for anyone.'* The correspondent who made this statement said that he was surprised that manufacturers of cars did not pay more attention to springing to enable solids to be more widely used.
November 1903	A medico writes to say that no doctor can afford to use pneumatics, on the showing of experiences with such tyres in the recent 1000-mile trial.
January 1905	Arrol Johnston cars are specially designed throughout for use with solid tyres.
January 1905	Albion advertise *'the solid tyred car.'*
June 1905	Report from Gloucestershire of general practitioners going back from pneumatics to solid tyres because of the time wasted on puncture repairs.

After this date, it is noticable that arguments about the relative merits of solids and pneumatics cease and letters about tyre performance change to a bragging match as to the good performance achieved from pneumatics!

March 1907	Palmer Tyres state that many of their customers have suffered no punctures at all in 10,000 miles of running.
July 1907	S. F. Edge's 24-hour single-handed run at Brooklands track, at an average of 66 m.p.h. Twenty-four tyres were changed during the run, on Dunlop beaded-edge equipment.

CHAPTER 6

Practical Progress

Two drawings from advertisements of the year 1900 are shown in (Figure 6·1). One shows a car tyre of wired-type, the second has a beaded-edge tyre. Both these tyres have completely smooth treads, unbroken by any groove or other pattern. Bearing in mind that the roads of those days, outside the towns, were of water-bound material, and of polished granite setts within the urban areas, it will be appreciated that wheel-grip was always precarious. When dry the road surface was loose and dusty, when wet it was muddy. We are apt to forget how hazardous was the road grip of these early cars. It needs some long forgotten precept to be restated, to bring the true situation to mind.

Rolls Royce made one revealing plea to the drivers of their early cars: '*Always remember that when a car is being braked it occupies twice as much road as when travelling normally!*' This instruction conjures up visions of cars with no front wheel brakes, still proceeding forward but with the rear wheels locked and with the line of the vehicle at 45° to the direction of travel.

Dry and wet skids were always happening. In fact they were included in the car instruction book as part of the driving technique of the day. Dr Fred Lanchester, of the Lanchester Brothers, wrote a driving manual which appeared in 1902. It describes how to sideslip and details various manoeuvres. As typical we may take 'The swing-around stop.':

"*The speed should be* 9-11 *m.p.h. The car is braked and at the same time steered. The tail comes round and the car describes a U-turn, ready to return on the other side of the road.*

It should on no account be attempted in the presence of other traffic

35

as it is a performance thoroughly disconcerting to other users of the road.

Remember that, whatever the state of the road, it is bad driving to navigate the car sideways."

It is not surprising, therefore, that motorists began to look around for ways of improving the grip of tyres on the road. Devices like the Parsons' chain, in practically the same form as we know it today, were not the complete answer under all-the-year-round conditions (Figure 6·2).

Leather jackets

The problem was, in fact, combined with two others; first the short life of the tread and secondly the liability of the tyre to puncture. An answer, in part, to all these problems came in leather over-jackets, two examples of these are illustrated (Figure 6·3). The first is the Grose 'non-slipping and puncture-proof band of studded leather,' the second is similar of Belgian design, marketed in England as 'The Perfecter'. It consisted of a leather outer jacket, strapped over the tyre by short leather links which passed between and encircled each spoke. The tread band of the device was covered with non-skid leather buttons, attached by steel rivets.

The fact that chrome leather was specified as the material for the manufacture of such devices gives an idea of the poor wear resistance of the rubber treads of those times.

These leather over-jackets for tyres found favour and continued to be patented and exploited for a decade. Two more of them, are shown (Figure 6·4), dated 1910. The Brooklands non-skid band was made of the usual chrome leather strips, rivetted together, with steel studs, which form a gripping pattern. The band was no longer strapped to the tyre. Instead its edges had spring steel hooks, secured by rivets, which were engaged with the hooked-over rim edge of the beaded-edge fitment. The second idea shown is French and proposed to use metal anchor strips, both on the shoulders and in a centre channel in the pattern.

Manufacturers take notice

The success of these devices in increasing the grip between tyre and road caused the tyre manufacturing industry to consider incorporating such features in the tyre itself. As was to happen with a number of tyre improvements in later years, the first initiative was taken by retreaders. In 1903 remoulded tyres appeared with an inlaid leather tread, complete with embedded steel studs (Figure 6·5). The next stage saw the same leather band and studs embodied in the

36

original moulding of a brand-new tyre. This occurred about 1905.

Such designs created such interest and gave the feeling of so much enhanced grip that their use was written into the regulations for the equipment of London taxicabs, which had to have studded tyres fitted to diagonal wheels well into the 'twenties.

The next stage of development came with the realisation that steel studs were not the only means for improving grip, and that what happened with a boot on the road at 3 m.p.h. was not necessarily true of tyres running at 20 m.p.h. or more.

There are two lines of thought observable from this point. The first replaces the steel studs with rubber buttons of the same size and distribution. Designs of this nature were especially attractive to the designers and makers of the early cycle tyre moulds. They found the addition of such studs a simple matter of drilling recesses, to a controlled depth, in the mould surface (Figure 6·6).

Rubber studs

The second attack on the problem was the provision of the first simple functional patterns. The Dunlop advertisement of 1906, with its very terse caption, speaks for itself (Figure 6·7). This tyre was produced without the use of a mould. The cross-slots were made by pressing metal bars or slugs into the soft rubber of the uncured tread and then wrapping or 'lapping' the tyre with a canvas binder, which held the slugs in position during the vulcanisation in open steam. A reconstruction of such a tyre showing the cross slots and the impression of the wrapping is shown (Figure 6·8).

Non-skid patterns

The fundamental problem of tyre building is the difficult one of making a toroidal-shaped casing out of rubbered fabric which comes in flat sheets.

Tyre building

In the early days of car tyre manufacture the flat material was a cross-woven canvas. This was capable of a certain amount of stretch from the flat to the bulged-out condition as the parts of the tyre were assembled on a toroidal shaped former. The former approximated to the size and shape of the inside of the finished tyre. It had to be capable of removal from the inside of the built-up tyre, without damage being done. Additionally some small final stretch had to be allowed for during moulding, when final slack in the casing would be taken up and the tread rubber forced into the mould pattern

This is no place to set out the detailed process for designing tyres or of the machines on which they are made. The I.R.I. monograph by E. C. Woods is a most useful summary of the design principles. As far as machinery is concerned, H. C. Pearson's 'Pneumatic Tires' published in New York in 1923, gives much detail, illustrated by drawings based on the patent specifications of inventors and manufacturers' instruction books of the time.

Variability in construction

So far as the performance of the finished tyres is concerned, much depended on the skill of the individual tyre builder. It was easy to lay down a hopeful method of tyre construction, and then to expect it to be followed slavishly by all the work-force of tyre makers. It was far more difficult to translate such a process into a reliable routine, carried out by groups of well-disciplined operatives, who would faithfully follow the process as laid down, hour after hour and day after day, for years on end. The need for faithful endeavour did not even finish with the men and women who built the tyres. The subsequent processes of inserting the airbag, or curing tube, on which the tyre was inflated in the mould, closing the mould, vulcanising and subsequently stripping the cover from the mould, were all subject to variability at every stage.

All these were operations where there were potential sources of danger to the tyre, in either its uncured state, before vulcanisation, or when hot and 'tender' straight from the moulding press.

It is especially important to bear in mind that the early car tyres, with which we are concerned, did not even have the support of a wire bead-foundation, but were built round a bead core of deformable vulcanite. In the course of careless handling during manufacture the bead core could be easily overstrained, or its adhesion to the casing round it damaged.

All this explains why the performance of early tyres was very variable. Neither the manufacturer nor the user could ever be certain what the strength of any particular casing might be. There were risks of early failure due to weaknesses in the construction of the tyres, brought about by slippage, displacement or overstrain of components during manufacture.

Racing evidence

Such differences in condition from one tyre to another were made visible in departures from the norm of performance. This was heightened as the demands made on the tyres, of which racing conditions were the most severe of all, increased. Documented evidence of the variability is available in the record of performance of the beaded-edge Dunlop tyres used in the famous 24-hour record run by S. F. Edge, with his Napier car, soon after the opening of Brooklands track in 1907.

"The earlier tyres (used during the evening and night) lasted longer than the later ones. Two tyres came off when the car had gone only a little distance past the replacement station, so that Edge had to run almost a complete lap on the rim.'

This experience was matched by that of many ordinary motorists, who occasionally had a rogue tyre which failed after negligible life.

Weftless cord

The greatest stride towards better uniformity of manufacture came when cross-woven canvas materials at last gave way, in the early 'twenties, to weftless, or virtually weftless, cord. The difficulty of shaping a casing, made up of pairs of crossed weftless plies, into a toroid of the shape of a moulded casing, was greatly eased. It now became possible to build the casings of such tyres as flat cylinders, in sizes where the rim diameter was large compared with the cross-sectional width. It was also possible to make truck tyres and the more difficult car sizes on a low-crowned former or shouldered drum, where only the bead area was shaped to something approaching its final toroidal section.

Breakaway from beaded-edge

In the years immediately before the First World War, there were evident signs of a movement to leave the beaded edge construction behind, so far as future developments of car tyres were concerned. The first field of work was the development of the demountable rim separate from the felloe (felly) or body of the wheel, into which the spokes fitted. If the rim was made separate then the tyre could be assembled to it and then fitted as a unit to the felloe of the wheel, which remained attached to the axle of the car.

The rim was usually arranged to contract inwards, being cut through at some part of its circumference so that the ends might be drawn radially inwards, by some kind of toggle mechanism, which broke the transverse joint and drew the two ends inwards (Figure 6·9). There were many well-engineered designs for doing this, with elaborate right and left-handed screw mechanisms for collapsing the rim. All were heavy, expensive and subject to corrosion, damage and neglect, during the relatively long periods between one tyre removal and the next.

The inevitable cheapening of the original designs took place and the split-rim type of fitment persisted in less worthy forms until the end of the 'twenties. The final form consisted of a one-piece, wambly rim base, contracted with a cheap three-armed screw-jack device, which was likely to detach itself with missile-like violence from the rim during operation. The rim itself was held in the expanded position by a crude turnbuckle type lock and was finally fixed in the expanded position by the jamming fit on the felloe, on which it was secured by small nut-attached sidepieces (Figure 6·10).

In spite of the crudity of such rim designs they had the advantage of enabling the wired-type tyre to be fitted and experience to be gained in its application to the automobile, ahead of the time when the well-base or drop-centre wheel became available for cars.

The move towards the detachable-rim wheel began in the U.S.A. where there had never been a complete devotion to beaded-edge constructions, and where much automobile tyre development had taken place in terms of the single-tube tyre, which was just a racing cycle construction strengthened up to the proportions necessary for a car.

CHAPTER 7

World War I

Those of us who have seen the motor industry live through two world wars know that events follow a certain predictable pattern. The two main features are. First a suppression of all development in the field of the pleasure or status automobile, so that there may be a concentration of all available effort on the needs of the war. The second feature is that the industry comes out of the war period bearing the imprint of change. This is the inevitable result of the impact of techniques born out of the needs of the times, which are carried forward into the post-war period.

World War I saw the motor industries of the combatant powers change over quickly to war production. This was not merely a switch from making private cars to building army trucks. It involved a wider swing-over, in which the established machine shop facilities of the industry, and the skilled labour force which they had at their disposal, were employed in producing a wide range of munition items.

The motor industry at war

So far as tyres were concerned, the emphasis was on the stepping up of the production of solid tyres for trucks. This was the main war effort, consuming many thousand tons of natural rubber, and calling for a large expansion of the manufacturing facilities available for the type of production.

Tyres and the war

Expansion of production led to the setting up by the Dunlop Rubber Company of a new factory. The original works at Aston Cross and the subsidiary factory at Manor Mills had been outgrown, and the industry now had to move out of the built-up urban area into the country on the outskirts of the city of Birmingham.

There were initial difficulties, as the new site, although only three miles from Aston Cross, was still without direct road connections with it. However, a new factory was planned and building began, with the ultimate objective of moving the whole manufacturing operation out into the Warwickshire fields. In the early stages some workers were ferried to and from the new factory in converted canal barges, in a morning and evening service connecting Fort Dunlop with Salford Bridge and Aston. Eventually a new road was cut, skirting the sandstone ridge of Gravelly Hill, so that tram tracks linked Aston, where the work force lived, with the new factory site, and opened up the Birches Green and Pype Hayes areas for subsequent building expansion.

The naming of the factory as Fort Dunlop remains a slight mystery. Industry moving into new areas was liable to imprint itself on place names as well as on modes of living. Cadbury's had pioneered with Bournville in the early 'eighties, which rapidly became more the name of a kind of cocoa than of the place. Lever Brothers similarly had Port Sunlight, up on Merseyside, the home of Sunlight soap.

The new Dunlop area, born in wartime, was named Fort Dunlop even before the building of the factory began, and was later linked with a slogan, 'The Stronghold of the British Tyre Industry' which had a good ring about it. To the workers in the factory, and to those who live around it, the Dunlop factory still remained 'the rubber', and it probably will always be so called.

Solid tyres Solid tyres do not really concern us, but some reference to them will be necessary, since their properties and their reaction to operating conditions have much in common with those under which pneumatic tyres have to serve.

The basic requirement of any tyre, solid or pneumatic, is that it should remain structurally sound until it is worn out. In both cases it is necessary to avoid overheating of the tyre. This is especially important in the solid tyre.

A solid tyre consists of a thick band of compounded rubber, attached to a steel base band which is carried on the wheel centre. This band of rubber is subjected, as it rolls, to rapid cycles of load and unloading. In the process each part of the circumference of the tyre is compressed and allowed to recover many times a second. For instance a 36″ solid tyre, at the permitted 20 m.p.h. revolves 3 times per second.

During the process of loading and release energy is absorbed in the tyre, since it is not perfectly resilient. Thus the work done in compressing the rubber as the load comes on is not all given up again when it is released. Furthermore, the energy is lost deep inside the mass of rubber making up the solid tyre, where it appears converted into heat.

Dissipation of heat is difficult, since rubber is a poor conductor of heat, consequently that generated within the mass of the tyre is slow in escaping.

When commercial transport ran on solid tyres, at speeds which were officially limited to 20 m.p.h., overheating failures in tyres were sometimes to be seen happening on the road. The process began with the overheating inside the tyre which has just been described. Under exceptional circumstances of overload or excessive speed, temperatures could be generated which led to the decomposition of the rubber at the centre of the mass of the tyre. The gaseous hydrocarbons, produced by the heat degradation of the rubber, were generated under pressure so that small pockets of gas were produced inside the tyre. As running continued the internal friction and the rubbing of the loosened parts of the tyre led to the gas eventually bursting out, usually through the wall of the tyre. As the vehicle ran along the road puffs of smoke could be seen, and smelled, emerging from the disintegrating tyre. Soon the failure developed further and the structure of the tyre broke down so that large pieces of the tread rubber became detached.

This problem of overheating inside the solid tyre was matched by an exactly parallel development of heat inside the treads of pneumatic tyres, when used at very high speeds on the road or in races. The problem was the same in both cases and the solution was common to both as will be described in a later chapter.

The First World War brought a still more difficult problem for the designer of solid tyres. This was as track supports for the new type of armoured fighting vehicle, capable of rapid cross-country travel, popularly known as the 'tank'. In its original form the vehicle travelled on long caterpillar tracks, running completely round the outer edges of its box-like form. The tracks were pressed against the ground by a series of solid tyred wheels, along the whole length of the ground contact, and rising high at each end of the armoured vehicle, to cover conditions experienced in climbing out of ditches or dropping into holes. The free portion of the tracks, running over the top of the box, was similarly guided by solid tyred 'idler' wheels.

Here was the first beginning of a new field of use for the solid tyre. One which involved speeds beginning at the 20 m.p.h. for which solid tyres had been designed, and which rapidly extended to faster and faster requirements as such vehicles became more mobile.

Overheating

Tank tracks

43

Cool-running compounds

The new demands stressed the need to understand how to produce cool-running solid tyre compounds. The problem was solved, and the knowledge once gained was then available in later years to meet the problem of cool-running treads for pneumatic tyres, as cars became fast enough and reliable enough to need them.

Synthetic rubber

In Germany, cut off from the outside world by a tight blockade, the problem of rubber supplies had to be faced. Stocks built up inside the country were not limitless and, by about the second year of the war, it was obvious that some provision had to be made for the manufacture of a substitute for natural rubber.

There was no difficulty about the basic mechanics of synthesising rubber-like polymers. Sir William Tilden, Professor of Chemistry at Mason College, Birmingham, had publicised the fact that he had accidentally synthesised rubber from a simple organic liquid, isoprene, which had been left in a bottle during the long vacation in 1882. This precise method, copying the rubber molecule exactly, was too expensive in its raw material and too time-consuming to be used under the urgent demands of wartime. So other, cheaper and more readily available materials, of the diolefine family, were examined, and it was found that the polymerisation of butadiene, using metallic sodium as a catalyst, to speed up the process, gave a workable method. The synthetic rubber so produced was known as 'buna'; the 'bu' from butadiene and 'na' from the chemical symbol for sodium, which is the first syllable of its Latin name natrium.

Buna rubber was produced on a scale of several thousand tons during the later stages of the German war effort, and it was used in the manufacture of solid tyres for their army trucks. As will be realised this was an exacting and demanding use for the new material. As has already been described, conditions inside a solid tyre demand rubber compounds of high resilience, if overheating is to be avoided.

Accelerators

The new material was immediately found to have great limitations compared with the natural rubber which it replaced. The process of combination with sulphur, involved in the vulcanising and moulding process, was found to be much slower. The German chemists were, therefore, compelled to look around for materials which could be added to the rubber mix, to speed up the rate of vulcanisation of buna with sulphur. Thus was born, of necessity, a new technique, involving what were known as 'accelerators of vulcanisation', soon shortened to 'accelerators'. These were usually organic nitrogen com-

44

pounds. Their use not only made it possible to make wartime solid tyres out of buna rubber, but the practice was carried over into peacetime, to make it possible to reduce cure times in articles made from natural rubber and so to increase the output of a given plant.

Linked with the development of accelerators came other organic additives to rubber compounds, aimed at reducing the attack of oxygen on the rubber, and so cutting down the rate of ageing. The first to be developed, in the 'twenties and 'thirties were the anti-oxidants, to be followed in turn by antiozonants.

The field of use where there was the greatest growth and development, during the war, was that of the aeroplane tyre.

Aeroplane tyres

The earliest aircraft designers had looked for the lightest possible tyre and wheel, which could be borrowed from existing uses. The first primitive machines, which were little more than powered box-kites, used tyres and wheels from bicycles and motorcycles. These ranges of tyres were already highly developed, were generally light in construction, and were capable of being used to carry considerable loads in relation to their weight. They did very well in their unaccustomed element.

By 1911-12 there were aeroplane tyres and wheels included in the Dunlop tyre catalogue. The tyres were still of motorcycle proportions, (Figure 7·1), and looked like it when in flight (Figure 7·2). The wheels were wire spoked with radial spoking. (Figure 7·3).

As aircraft developed, and as under wartime conditions the first production lines were set up for their building, new ranges of tyres and wheels were designed, to meet the exact requirements of the designers. The new aero-tyres tended to be larger in section and smaller in relative wheel diameter than the cycle or motorcycle tyre. These proportions were a compromise, based on the need for a certain sectional width, but coupled with a requirement that the total frontal area of the tyres should be kept down, to reduce the air resistance of the whole plane.

It was soon found that wire spoked wheels produced high windage drag when spun in air, and that it was beneficial to cover the spokes with a light fabric fairing, to reduce drag. Such tyres, used always on grass aerodromes or fields, presented no tyre wear problems. Treads could be thin and light, and patterns were either omitted or restricted to the simplest shallow grooves. The main need was for cushioning, against the unevenness of the ground and against the shock of touch down. High deflection was essential and it was soon realised that the aeroplane tyre had to be capable of being crushed in section, completely down to the rim, in a heavy landing, without suffering any damage.

In this period the Palmer Company, with their pioneer use of cord constructions, and with sophisticated apparatus for making such tyres, built up a reputation in the aircraft field.

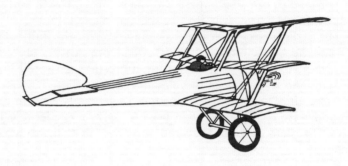

CHAPTER 8

Simpler & Better

The end of World War I saw all the pent-up development which had been worked out during the war years beginning to appear in everyday tyres.

At the first post-war motor shows all the cars were still on beaded-edge tyres. The 1920 exhibition was so large that it filled both Olympia and the White City, and over one hundred distinct makes of car were on show. By the 1922 show Dunlop had a wired-type car tyre, fitted on a detachable-flange rim. From that stage the change-over in tyre practice was rapid. In 1924 Dunlop were able to announce that their standard range of tyres was now of the wired-type and that they proposed in future to make only one beaded-edge size.

This Dunlop development went further than the Americans, in that the wired-type cover was made with relatively narrow, fairly flexible beads, so that the ideal, one-piece, well-base rim could be brought into use. It meant too that the car designer might have the tyre and wheel unit of extreme simplicity, which had been enjoyed by the cycle world for so long.

It was on such light but strong equipment that the Austin '7' and the Morris 'Cowley' and other epoch-making British and European cars were introduced. At first there was some scepticism about the safety of such tyres, especially when deflated after a puncture. A racing driver, Paul Dutoit, carried out reassuring demonstrations for Dunlop, to prove that there was no danger of tyres coming off the well-base wheel on deflation (Figure 8·1). However, about 1927, in the light of further experience, the originally deep wells of such wheels were made somewhat shallower, without rendering fitting too difficult.

Michelin pursued the safety idea to the logical conclusion, with a wheel which had a well for only half its circumference, and which had a safety pad fitted to the valve-stem of the tube thus blocking the centre portion of the half-well, when the tyre was in position (Figure 8·2).

47

British designers took the lead in exploiting the well-base rim, which was well-established by the mid-'twenties. French engineers followed, beginning in 1928, and in that year, Ford were the first American firm to adopt the 'drop-centre' rim, as they called it.

Low pressures in inch sizes

A feature of the new well-base wired tyres was that they were designed to run at relatively low pressures. The first tyres used on heavy cars, in the early years of the century, were designed to operate at 90 or even 100 lb/sq. in. inflation pressure. As development proceeded this had been reduced to a general level of 60-70 lb/sq. in. by the beginning of the 'twenties. The new range of well-base sizes was run at 30-35 lb/sq. in. But, to have a given carrying capacity or load, the low pressure tyre must have a larger section. This follows since the loading of a tyre onto the road is rather like floating a boat on water, the tyre sinks onto the road surface, until the contact area is such that the reaction of the road, measured as contact area x inflation pressure, is equal to the load carried (there is a small proportion of the load carried by the walls of the inflated tyre, but otherwise the statement is true).

Marking

The other feature of the new tyres was that dimensions were given in inches instead of millimetres, and the new tyres fitted inch-size rims. The whole size-marking had an English look about it and was reasonably logical, although it was not possible to determine, by casual inspection, that the popular tyre size marked 27 x 4.40 was based on a 19 inch wheel.

The coming of cord

The second revolution of the years when the tyre industry straightened itself out after the war was the introduction of cord constructions, in place of canvas, in car tyres. As mentioned earlier, this had been standard practice in cycle tyres for thirty years, but it had not been necessary or expedient to extend the cord principle to larger tyres, and the factory problems of handling large quantities and wide rolls had discouraged moves in that direction.

As speeds of cars increased, and their reliability and usefulness were extended, designers began to look for facilities to make better tyres. The cord construction was an obvious step forward, as had been proved in the cycle field. The basic principle has already been outlined in Chapter 3. To recapitulate; 'the cross-over knuckles of woven material are eliminated, so that internal chafing and disruption do not take place during the repeated cycles of loading and unloading to which each part of the tyre is subjected as it runs under load.'

48

Figure 7.1
Tyres and wheels of cycle type and
proportions used on early aircraft.

Figure 7.2, below right.
The Blackburn 'Mercury', 1911.

Figure 7.3, below.
Early wire wheel for aircraft with
radial spoking.

Figure 8.1.
Racing driver, Paul Dutoit, demonstrating that Dunlop wired-type tyres, on well-base wheels, do not come off the rim when run deflated. The car is an Alvis 'Firefly' and it is being driven in tight circles, at Brooklands, with a flat rear tyre.

Figure 8.2.
Michelin's safety wheel of the 'twenties', with a well for only half of the circumference. On inflation, a safety pad on the valve blocks up the well and prevents the tyre leaving the rim.

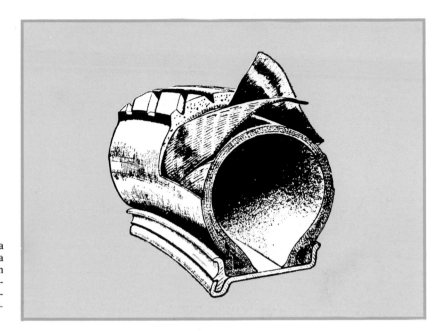

Figure 8.3
Dunlop, in 1922, changes over to a wired type tyre construction, with a woven cord casing. The tyre shown is on a straightside rim with a detachable flange. Wellbase, single-piece wheels became rapidly accepted.

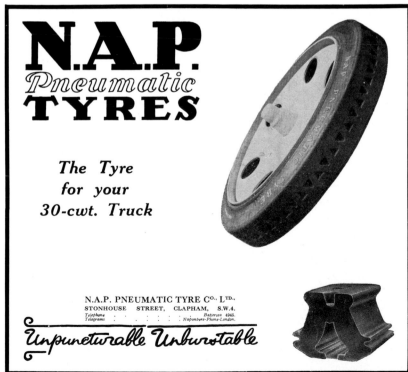

N.A.P.
Pneumatic
TYRES

*The Tyre
for your
30-cwt. Truck*

N.A.P. PNEUMATIC TYRE C⁰., L™.,
STONHOUSE STREET, CLAPHAM, S.W.4.
Telephone . . . . . *Battersea* 4945.
Telegrams . . . . . *Naponteyre-Phone-London.*

Unpuncturable Unburstable

Figure 8.4.
The Killen N.A.P. (normal air pressure) tyre. This so called "pneumatic" tyre was simply a solid, with extra deflection and cushioning obtained by putting cavities into its structure. As indicated in this advertisement its use was restricted to vehicles of low load capacity.

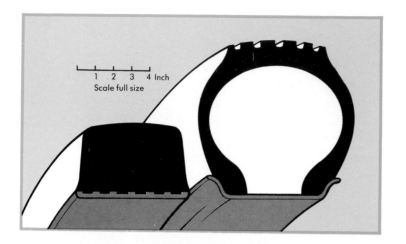

Figure 8.5,
Comparative sections of a typical 100 millimetre solid tyre and of the 8.25 inch low-pressure pneumatic tyre which replaced it.

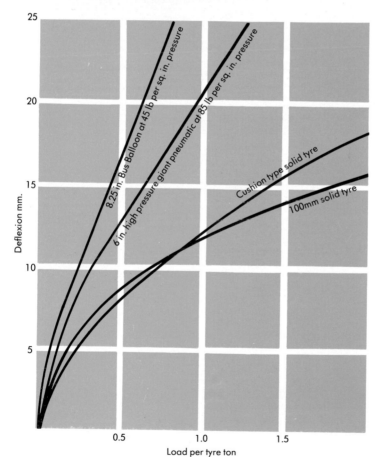

Figure 8.6,
The difference in load/deflection relations between solid, cushion, high-pressure and low-pressure pneumatic tyres. The solid tyres can be seen to have greatly reduced cushioning capacity as load is increased.

Two types of material are available, the completely weftless, produced by rubbering a warp of cords drawn direct from a creel, and the 'woven weftless', in which the weft threads are reduced to spaced-out 'picks' of fine gauge thread which make it possible to handle the material as a self-supporting fabric.

The Palmer company, operating the basic patents of their American founder, had used cord constructions for aeroplane tyres and had various complex machines available for building tyres of weftless construction, by laying a single rubbered cord on to a toroidal former, to form successive plies of the casing. These processes were ahead of their time and were relatively expensive in operation, so that they never seem to have been developed into large volume manufacture.

The bulk of European production of car tyres, which was based on canvas at the beginning of the twenties, soon changed over to cord construction. The Dunlop tyre of 1922, on its straightside rim, had a cord casing (Figure 8·3). 'The Autocar' in 1921, comments on the rapid growth in popularity of cord-built casings.

This change in the basic casing material brought an increase in the number of cycles of load and unload which the tyre would withstand before failure from fatigue. The change tends to be remembered as having produced a tenfold increase in casing life, from say an average of 3,000 to 30,000 miles. Checking up on the mileages quoted by bragging motorists in the correspondence columns of the 'twenties, it seems that this recollection is exaggerated, but it is plain that a very substantial improvement in casing life, of the order of 3 to 1, or even 5 to 1, was actually achieved. What is certain is that the coming of cord constructions meant that the casing could now be depended upon to outlast the tread.

We have come a long way on the course of this history of tyre development without mention of the fact that tyre design is always a matter of striking the most acceptable compromise, in the light of the requirements of the time, between a number of inter-related and often conflicting properties. This is illustrated in the situation presented by the introduction of weftless cord material into car tyre casings. Although the improved fatigue performance of the new construction was accepted with gratitude, there were many complaints, at first, of the reduction in vehicle comfort, which went hand-in-hand with the change from canvas to cord. The canvas tyre, with its built-in internal friction (as the threads of the cross-woven fabric sawed over

More life—less comfort

49

each other during running) acted as its own shock-absorber or damper. It was a property valued on the primitive cars of the 'twenties, with their well-lubricated leaf-springs and rudimentary friction shock-absorbers. On such a vehicle, the removal from inside the tyres of the internal friction which they had formerly possessed made the car noticeably less comfortable. Inevitably, however, the progress represented by the improved reliability of the cord tyre was quickly accepted as the paramount feature, and shock absorber systems were improved to take over that part of the work which the tyre had ceased to do.

The increased casing life, made available by the change to cord constructions, would not have been fully beneficial had it not been for the fortunate introduction, at about the same time, of means of making a parallel improvement in the life of the tread rubber of the tyre.

Carbon-black and tread wear

Up to this time, tread compounding had been a matter of making up a mixture of rubber and sulphur, ready for vulcanisation by heat, and adding such other 'drugs' as had been found empirically to give enhanced properties, or to speed up the vulcanisation, or even to give an acceptable colour to the mix. Zinc oxide, litharge and magnesia were used in this way. Other materials, such as china clay and lithopone, were used simply as diluents or loading materials, to cheapen the rubber mix. As a result of the use of large quantities of zinc oxide, the tread and walls of the tyres of those days were white or cream in colour.

About 1910 the Silvertown Rubber Company, in London, discovered that the carbon black used for printers' ink could be used not only to colour rubber, but to produce a marked improvement in its resistance to wear on the road. The carbon black used was produced by the burning of hydrocarbon gases in the old batswing burners. The flame was allowed to impinge on cool iron plates or channels, in the form of a slowly moving conveyor, on the surface of which the smoke from the incomplete combustion of the gas was allowed to collect. This crude process has subsequently been improved, by carrying out the combustion in a scientifically designed furnace and using modern dust-collecting apparatus to gather in the products of combustion.

The large-scale production of gas-black, as it was called, for industrial use, started in the U.S.A., where suitable natural gas for burning occurred widely in the oil-field areas. The early communication of the Silvertown experience to the Diamond Rubber Co., in the U.S.A. led to the rapid development of the use of carbon black in rubber mixes, throughout the American industry, and generally throughout the world. The Diamond Co., incidentally, was soon absorbed into the B. F. Goodrich organisation.

Colloidal carbon black, produced as a smoke, has a fantastically small particle size, with a correspondingly enormously large specific surface. Put into ordinary language the particles making up one gramme of the type of black used in tyre treads have a total surface area of about one hundred square metres. This fine-particle carbon was found to fit into the structure of the rubber molecule, increasing its internal friction or hysteresis, but at the same time putting up its resistance to abrasion by a factor of ten.

Linked with these changes in tread compounding, came the introduction into ordinary rubber practice of the organic accelerators of vulcanisation, first devised, as already mentioned, to improve the slow-curing properties of the synthetic rubbers used in Germany at the end of the first world war. These materials soon became much more than speeders-up of processing. It was found that their introduction into a basic mix of rubber, sulphur, zinc oxide and carbon black made it possible to produce a range of properties in the final vulcanised mix, which could be selected to match exactly the requirements of various parts of the tyre.

Accelerators

The obvious change was the coming of the black tyre. After a transitional change during which sidewalls were still white or cream, capped with a black tread, the new material invaded the whole product and a new range of properties came to the tyre.

During World War I the pneumatic tyre for heavy trucks and buses began to be developed. By 1917, Goodyear in the U.S.A. had reached the stage of development where a transcontinental motor express was running from coast to coast, in fourteen days or less, on pneumatic truck tyres. They were frank enough to admit that much of the payload carried by the vehicle had to be spare tyres.

Pneumatic tyres for heavy vehicles

In Europe the parallel development had to wait for the end of the war. In the interim the solid tyre had a last fling, especially in the form of soft, cushion tyres with increased deflection and comfort. One of these, the N.A.P., the initials standing for 'normal air pressure', claimed quite wrongly to be a pneumatic tyre and bore engravings to

51

that effect on its walls. Such tyres were confined to relatively light loads, such as the 30 cwt truck of the advertisement (Figure 8·4).

The first two truck sizes, 36 x 6 and 40 x 8, appeared in the Dunlop price list in 1921, and with them a range of high pressure giant tyres, for commercial vehicles was launched.

Development of the giant tyre range was rapid and pneumatic truck tyres became accepted as the standard fitment for passenger and the better goods vehicles. By 1928 Dunlop's Technical Director was lecturing to the Institute of Automobile Engineers on the use of the new tyres, and quoting fleet average mileages between 8,400 and 40,200 miles.

The drawing (Figure 8·5) illustrates the comparative sectional sizes of a typical solid tyre and of the giant pneumatic tyre which replaced it, for the same load.

The graph (Figure 8·6) illustrates the difference in load/deflection characteristics between four types of truck tyre: solid, cushion, the first high pressure giant pneumatic and the low pressure range which soon followed.

The point to be made is that comfort depends on the rate of increase of tyre deflection with increase in load. The solid tyre, as will be seen from the graph, was poor on cushioning because, when normally loaded, it was already compressed almost to the limit, so that extra shock loads were not well cushioned. With the pneumatic tyres, the deflection continues to increase at a uniform rate as the load is raised above the normal level, and the cushioning properties continue to be good as shock loads are met.

Brakedrum heat

One tyre problem, encountered in the late 'twenties, was that of brakedrum heat, which caused a considerable number of tyre bursts on the trucks.

A truck design engineer made his brakedrums as large as possible, to give high retarding effort and long brakelining life. As a result the outside of the brake-drums fitted closely inside the rims of the wheels. At the points of minimum clearance there was often contact, for instance between the valve stem, or the gutter in which it lay, and the outer surface of the drum. This led to the rapid transfer of large quantities of heat from the brakedrum to the rim, and hence to the base of the bead and to the valve and the tube and flap.

The result was to cause the thermal degradation of the rubber compounds, resulting in tube failures and in disintegration of the tyre bead structure, resulting in bead bursts. These conditions were too severe to be met by any changes in the rubber compounds used.

The basic cause of the trouble was clear, and sensible standards were soon laid down on an industry basis, for clearances between the outer surface of the brakedrum and the inner surface of the wheel. It may be said, however, that as vehicles continued to become heavier, and faster, with corresponding increased demands on their brakes, young engineers have looked, from time to time, at the available space for bigger brakedrums, and sometimes learned the same lesson over again, by courting disaster and cutting down clearances.

CHAPTER 9

The Beginnings of Tyre Science

By the mid 'twenties the pneumatic tyre had arrived at a stage where development had to pass from the hands of the traditional 'old rubber dog', whose empirical knowledge had built up the industry, to the new tyre scientist. Days of hit-and-miss designs, inspired hunches, and secret compounding formulae which were kept in George's head, were fast passing. The industry began, immediately after the war, to recruit teams of young men, whose skills could be realigned to deal with new types of problems.

The chemists had a good start here, because they had a scientific regime, already established, which could be adapted easily to deal with the problems of tyre compounds, accelerators of vulcanisation and anti-oxidants; and which could show rapid evidence of the benefits of technical control and research. In the field of tyre design and testing, there was less immediately available know-how and the industry depended on the skill and vision of its senior staff, in recruiting young men to do new work, and in redirecting skills acquired in other fields, to the development of the pneumatic tyre.

Dunlop leads

Typical of this development was the Dunlop team of the 'twenties, recruited by the Technical Director, W. H. Paull, who had come to Dunlop with the take-over of the Clipper Tyre Co. He found a chief chemist, Dr D. F. Twiss, from a local technical college, who soon established a world-wide name in rubber, and who continued for many years to pioneer rubber chemistry, pure and applied, and to investigate new processes.

The team dealing with the physics and mechanics of the tyre was headed by a young mathematician from Nottingham University,

Albert Healey, supported by a handful of other young men of his generation. The first task of this team was to bring into the factory a measure of scientific control, and to tackle a number of basic problems which arose in the manufacturing process. Thus a simple apparatus, robust enough for use in factory control, was devised to monitor the plasticity of masticated rubber. Also, a pendulum device was designed to test blocks of cured rubber compounds, to determine their resilience, and the power loss in them, over a cycle of load and unload, corresponding to that experienced in a tyre running on the road. Fundamental work was begun on the laboratory measurement of the abrasion resistance of the rubber compounds used in tyre treads, and the techniques to be followed to ensure that the results should line up with those obtained on the road.

The most valuable work carried out by the team was a study of the tyre and the part it played in the suspension system of a car. Results of the project were published in the world's first technical paper on the pneumatic tyre. This was 'The Tyre as a part of the Suspension System', given as a lecture by Healey at centres of the Institution of Automobile Engineers, in November 1924. The paper, with its appendices and diagrams, occupied 100 pages of he Proceedings of the Institution," in 1925, and was the first published paper taking the tyre to be a part of the car. It thus broke completely new ground. It also provoked some of the established automobile engineers, whose ire was aroused that a mere mathematician should invade their territory and poke fun at some of their established practices. In the discussion, for example, it is recorded that Healey was criticised because he showed graphs in which tyre deflections measured in millimetres were set against loads in hundredweights.

However, the lecture was supported by experiments with an elegant model demonstrating the movement of the axle, at various speeds of excitation by tyre revolution, and showing the way in which the so-called 'unsprung' mass vibrated between the chassis and the road.

The lecture had an appendix of tyre data, including load/deflection curves and road contact diagrams, such as had never before been available to the car designer. With this sample of information came an offer to collaborate with vehicle design engineers, in any way they wished. Here was the first beginnings of a collaboration, which was to grow steadily as the years passed by and which resulted eventually

The tyre as part of the car

55

in extremely close links between Dunlop and car designers, on a world wide basis.

Factory engineering

A word should be said about the engineering side of the industry, although this book cannot attempt to give a complete, or even coherent account, of this side of the business where parallel advances were taking place. In Europe the development of tyre making machinery and tyre moulding plant tended to be done either inside the local factory or by engineering teams closely allied to the industry and working to instructions. In the U.S.A. specialist organisations, designing, making and selling rubber machinery, supplied the very large and generally simplified demands of a mass-production industry. By the mid-'twenties these American firms had links with European firms, and plant such as the Banbury internal rubber mixer were being made under licence.

Early pattern design

An interesting illustration (Figure 9·1) is from the 'Autocar' of autumn 1922, and shows thumbnail sketches of ten tread patterns used, at that date, on car tyres. Most of these patterns are just different from each other. The idea of seeking increased fore-and-aft grip is apparent, but that is about all. Some of them, like the Goodyear design, are very good in their combination of grip and resistance to irregular wear. Others, especially those with sharp-edged transverse bars which dominate more than half the designs, have been designed in ignorance, to wear out wastefully and irregularly.

At that time Dunlop designs had already begun to be worked out on the basis of a slow-wearing circumferential rib, or ribs, in the centre, with angled cross-slots for drainage and to give fore-and-aft grip. The 'traction' pattern, as it was called, was very successful and was one of the first designs which attempted to combine long wear with good grip (Figure 9·2).

A sketch in the last Chapter, (Figure 8·2) shows how such a tread pattern was combined with the use of a wired-type bead, weftless cord, and on a straightsided rim.

The 'traction' pattern belonged to the era of the medium-high-pressure tyre. As the low-pressure 'balloon' tyre arrived, in the mid-'twenties, there was an attempt to combine it with a new type of flexible, broken pattern. The Goodyear diamonds were a success here. Attempts by other makers to use square blocks (Figure 9·3), at low pressures, in the 20·30 lb/sq. in. range, led to violent irregular wear. It was soon found necessary to join up the isolated blocks again

Figure 9.1
Ten different car tyre patterns from the Motor Show of 1922. All are in beaded-edge form. Most of them concentrate on fore-and aft grip.

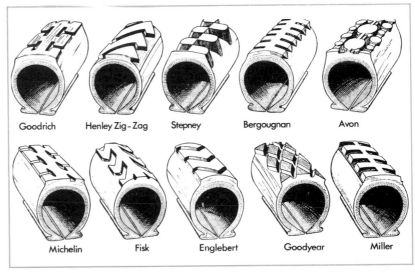

Goodrich   Henley Zig-Zag   Stepney   Bergougnan   Avon

Michelin   Fisk   Englebert   Goodyear   Miller

Figure 9.2 Far Right.
Dunlop 'traction' pattern, 1922, combining a long-wearing centre rib with angled sidestuds for grip.

Figure 9.3 Below Centre.
Dunlop 'triple stud' pattern, 1927, with excellent grip but a tendency to irregular wear unless the blocks were joined up circumferentially.

Figure 9·4.
Drawing from 'Motor Cycle', 1928, showing the study of pattern movement of a tyre, which is pressed upwards against the lower surface of a glass trolley, on which the tread rolls.

Figure 10.1, far left.
The '90' tyre of 1931, with ribbed, silent running, long wearing tread, with small transverse notches to improve fore-and-aft grip.

Figure 10.2, left.
The first tyre with teeth along the pattern edge to increase road grip.

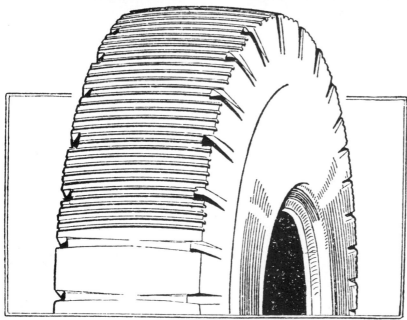

Figure 10.3,
The Tecalemit system, 1934, of cutting transverse slots in worn treads, to give renewed road grip.

Figure 10.4A, right.
Englebert's 'A.D.' (antiderapant) tread pattern, 1935, with bladed sidestuds and intricate surface pattern

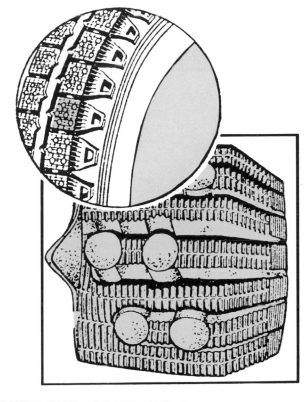

Figure 10.4B, below right.
Details from Michelin's patent of their pattern with the side-studs broken into a series of rubber blades.

Figure 10.5, below.
Dunlop pattern with combination of slots, teeth on rib edges, and variable pitch pattern units, to reduce noise.

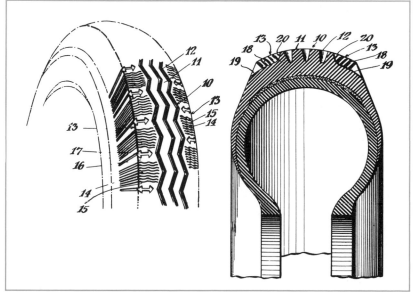

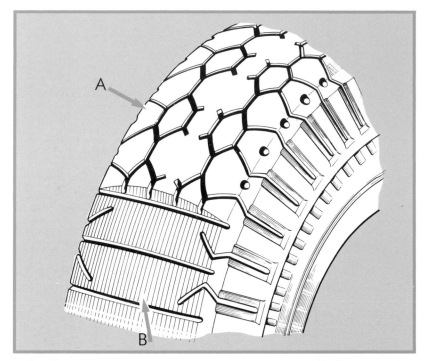

Figure 10.6
The Seiberling Duo-tread as used by the Avon Company.
The arrow 'A' indicates the original moulded tread pattern with holes passing through the tread rubber from side to side. 'B' shows the tyre in an ideal half-worn state, with the transverse holes broken through to form the basis of a second tread pattern.

Figure 10.7A and B, centre.
Tests carried out in 1930, on horse drawn vehicles with equal loads, showing the greatly reduced effort needed to pull a cart on pneumatic tyres, compared with the old iron-shod vehicle.

Figure 10.8
Tests in 1930 on the first British tractor to be fitted with pneumatic tyres.

forming basically longitudinal ribs, which gave even and slow wear.

The little sketch (Figure 9·4) of the tyre physicist, studying a rolling tyre, through a glass road, comes from a popular article which was all that was published about the first work of this kind ever done.

Solid tyres and racing tyres are two fields of tyre service which are a long way apart, but where the work of Healey and his small team contributed answers to what turned out to be the same problem, in one experimental technique.

Solid Tyres and Racing

When a rubber tread is loaded and unloaded, the energy absorbed on loading is not all returned on the unload. This is because the rubber compound is not perfectly elastic and there is a loss, or hysteresis, in the cycle of load and unload. Compounding the rubber with carbon black, to improve its resistance to wear, increases the amount of energy which is lost in this way. Lost energy becomes degraded into heat, and, as rubber is a poor conductor of heat, the rubber rises in temperature internally.

In the case of a solid tyre this meant that high temperatures, of the order of 150°C, developed internally so that the rubber compound used to break down, first to a liquid and then to a pocket of gas inside the mass of the rubber, as has already been described.

The race-tyre story was somewhat similar. Here the heat build up during running took place within a relatively thin tread. Also the conditions of heat generation were much more severe, as the speed was so much higher, and the number of cycles of loading and unloading followed each other at a rate of about 20 per second, at 100 m.p.h. The result was the same as with the solid tyre. There was breakdown of the rubber compounds and the formation of a sticky mess where formerly there were good rubber compounds bonding the tread to the casing.

But the race tyre does not wait to the stage where it emits puffs of smoke to show that all is not well. Centrifugal force demands that the tyre tread shall be held firmly to the casing, to prevent the tyre from being flung apart. When the adhesion of tread to casing was reduced, by overheating, at the base of the tread, the tread loosened and was thrown off, either completely as a band, or in small pieces. Tread-stripping was one of the hazards of motor racing in the 'twenties and one of the first spectacular successes of the work of W. H. Paull's team was to make a tyre which could be guaranteed not to lose its tread when run fast.

High speed test machine

To this end, in the middle 'twenties, Dunlop built a high speed test machine, so that experiments might be undertaken to find out about tyre performance at high speeds. The machine was home-made, designed on the site, and built at minimum cost largely from components at hand. When complete it was used in a fundamental programme of research on the factors affecting the performance of tyres at high speed. The machines used in routine testing ran generally at 50 m.p.h., although one pair of drums had been speeded up to 80 m.p.h. The new machine took over at about 90 m.p.h. and ran up to 150 m.p.h. Later its capacity was stretched to cover 'world speed record' work up to 200 m.p.h.

The attack on the problem was two-pronged. First of all there was a highly skilled investigation of the connection between the elastic properties of rubber compounds and the temperatures generated in tyres made from them. The basic laboratory work was done with a rapid impact machine, which struck a rubber block and measured the rebound (the time of the cycle being chosen to correspond with that in a tyre running at 30 m.p.h. on the road). The striker was carried on a pendulum beam and the machine was rapidly established as a most useful device for testing and controlling the properties of rubber mixes. Subsequently a miniaturised version called the Tripsometer, was designed and marketed commercially. It took very small samples and made it possible to investigate the properties of rubber taken from top and base of a tread, thus providing an indication of the cure gradient in the sample.

From work on the high speed test machine, with actual full-scale tyres, the effect of rubber compound, casing construction, and of thickness on running temperature were investigated. It was found, early in the work, that the tyre as it ran on the machine could exhibit standing waves, beginning at the point where the tyre left the drum surface and extending back round the tyre. It was observed that the formation of these waves was accompanied by a large increase in the power required to drive the tyre round. As this power went into the tyre there was the inevitable hysteresis loss, so that the tyre heated up rapidly and very soon stripped its tread. This led to a subsidiary programme of work in which the effect of tread thickness, casing construction, and inflation pressure on wave formation, were determined.

The results achieved in these experiments, over a period of only a

58

few months, showed again the truth of the adage that once a system of measurement is available, in any field, progress begins to be made.

There is a story which Sir George Beharrell, one time Chairman and Managing Director of the Dunlop Rubber Company, used to tell, of J. G. Parry Thomas, the Brooklands racing driver, undertaking to test tyres for Dunlop on the track. A contract was drawn up setting a flat rate for the testing with additional bonuses for each tyre which was run to the point where the tread stripped. At first all went well and the results were rewarding to Thomas. But, with the improvements in running temperature, which came as a result of pendulum-testing of the rubber compounds and the machine checking of tyre constructions, the situation changed. Thomas came to see Sir George and asked to be released from his contract, as he was no longer making enough money to pay for the petrol that was being used! This may sound like a tall story, but it is true.

The result, so far as Brooklands was concerned, was a great improvement in the safety of racing tyres. Tread-stripping, both on this track and elsewhere, was practically eliminated, except when the heaviest cars were driven in gruelling events.

This work then led to the coming of reliable race tyres and saw the end of improvisation in that most hazardous field. E. A. D. Eldridge used to tell how he prepared tyres for his 21-litre Fiat, for short sprint races and for attacks on the World's flying kilometre and mile records. (In those days of the early 'twenties the speed was in the range 130-140 m.p.h.) His practice was to buy a set of the best commercial car tyres and to set about buffing their treads away, to convert them into special sprint equipment. The method was to buff until the tread was completely removed and the first traces of fabric came into view. At this stage the tyre surface was tidied up and the tyres were safe to run at world-record speed.

Such makeshifts gave way to properly designed, thin-tread sprint tyres, with both casing and tread chosen to run cool, and with adequate strength built into the beads or cover edges to resist high centrifugal force effects at speed. Tyres of this kind were used by Parry Thomas and by Malcolm Campbell at Pendine in 1925-27. The technique was further extended to cover the Sunbeam Company's special twin-engined car, which was built to go to Daytona Beach, Florida, at the beginning of 1927, to attempt the first record at over 200 m.p.h., in the hands of Major H. O. D. Segrave.

The safe race tyre

World speed tyres

59

A graph contained in a report, was given to Segrave, summing up the properties of the tyres with which he had been equipped. The measurements, based solely on machine tests, showed that at just over 200 m.p.h. the rate of heating and power consumption of the tyres becomes so rapid that they will have a life of only a few seconds. At that stage no one knew what was the relation between these temperatures, measured on a machine, in an enclosed test house and running on a curved steel drum, and those likely to be attained on the sands of Daytona Beach. Major Segrave was assured that on the evidence available the tyres should successfully run at 200 m.p.h. Happily they did so, and the new record was established at an average speed of 203 m.p.h. with no sign of tyre trouble.

CHAPTER 10

Tread Patterns in The Thirties

The 'thirties saw a continuation of work on tread patterns, which had begun in the second half of the 'twenties. There were problems in various directions. At this time, using natural rubber and with relatively unsophisticated compounding ingredients, the rubber compounders were in trouble with tread cracks developing in the circumferential grooves of tread patterns. 'We can provide you', they said, 'with high wear-resistance treads, if you, the designers, will avoid the use of circumferentially-grooved patterns.' Unfortunately the appeal came just at the time when the tyre designers had come to the conclusion that if irregular wear was to be avoided and tread life assured, it was essential that patterns should have a basis of ribs with circumferential grooves between them. So compromise came into the situation and the treads were designed with ribs and grooves. But the grooves were often made less testing on the rubber compound, by the inclusion of intermittent platforms in their length.

Pattern compromises

The designer, for his part, also had his problems. On city streets, polished by traffic, the plain ribbed 'silent' patterns did give an almost complete absence of tyre noise, and so satisfied the designers of Rolls Royce and other town carriages in this, to them, important respect. But, in the wet, such tyres with natural rubber treads did not have good grip on braking, and sliding shunts into the backs of the vehicles ahead were not unknown. Such patterns as Dunlop's '90', of 1931, gained some slight extra fore-and-aft grip from the small notches in the sides of the circumferential ribs (Figure 10·1).

Grip was improved in two ways by the middle of the decade. The

Indented ribs

61

first improvement was achieved by making some of the edges of the ribs indented or 'toothed'. These teeth had a component of fore-and-aft grip and the total length of the edge of the pattern was greatly increased. This type of design (Figure 10·2), was invented by Dunlop and patented by them in the names of F. G. W. King, L. J. Lambourn and Frank Jones. It had a considerable psychological appeal to the motorist and the practice of designing 'tyres with teeth to grip the road' was widely copied, on both sides of the Atlantic, so that patterns of this kind became a new standard look for tyres.

The Knifecut   The other pattern improvement was based on the idea of a multi-bladed squeegee, the effect being produced by knifecutting the surface of the tyre tread. The original patent here was by Tecalemit, in France, who introduced tyre slicing as a means of restoring the grip of smooth tyres. The patent was no. 427,143 dated 1934. It described the use of a bacon-slicer type of machine, controlled to give a predetermined depth of cut in the worn tread of the tyre (Figure 10·3).

The process was applied to bald, worn-out tyres. It really did work and was quickly found not just to give some restoration of the wet grip, which the tyre had when new, but an outstandingly good grip at that. As a result the sprint hill-climb motorist, and the sprint speed trial entrant began to bring new tyres, with full tread pattern, to be given the 'Pneugrippa' treatment, as it was called. The practice rapidly spread to tyres used on wet racing days.

The next step was the embodiment of the knifecut principle into the new moulded tyre, as part of the designed pattern, instead of slicing up, at random, the designs which had been carefully worked out to produce a planned balance of tread wear and grip.

Two continental patterns are shown (Figure 10·4), produced between 1934-36, in which the sidestuds were provided with moulded knifecuts, produced by steel blade inserts in the production mould. The Englebert tyre, produced in Belgium, by what was then a family firm, was an extremely adventurous excursion into the new and the untried. The Michelin bladed tread was launched by another family firm, with a reputation for a succession of novelties, and their pattern 'aux lamelles' (with blades), started a fashion which was sufficiently sound in its technical foundation to last for many decades.

Dunlop produced a more restrained version of the idea in 1937, in which the blades were located in one edge of the outer and intermediate ribs of the design. This brought the knifecuts into the

62

main load-bearing area of the tread, where they could be most effective in increasing grip.

The mechanism by which these knifecuts in the tread were able to produce extra grip on wet roads was visualised at that time as though a multiple-bladed squeegee, or wiper blade, were sweeping the water off the road surface, giving the tyre the essential dry-road grip.

Acceptance of the new idea in pattern design was slow in the U.S.A. One maker took the idea to the limit and produced a tyre, moulded with a completely bald tread, which was treated before sale with a closely spaced system of shoulder to shoulder sliced cuts. It does not appear, however, to have been too successful, as its appearance was strange and was not the kind of tyre which the motorist could produce with pride at the golf club.

The fact that it was some years before the American market became interested in knife-cut treads is shown by the fact that they are called 'sipes' in the U.S.A., after the inventor of a system of knifecutting, Harry E. Sipe, as late as 1939.

Road noise

In the 'thirties, as roads became smoother and as the proportion of saloon cars which were quieter running increased, the motorist became conscious, for the first time, of the part of the vehicle noise which was contributed by tyres.

It became possible to identify the circular-saw-like 'sing' which came from the impact of regularly-spaced tread pattern studs on the road. This singing noise, which rose and fell in pitch as speed changed, was reduced by the general trend towards ribbed tread designs, which has just been described. But enough regular impulses remained in the pattern such as the teeth and the new slots or knifecuts, to constitute a source of tyre 'sing'.

The attack on this problem was to remove the regular distribution of the pattern elements and to redesign the layout detail of the pattern so as to have 'variable pitch'. Thus the single pattern unit of constant length was replaced by three units, one long, one medium and one short in length. These units were made up as diecastings, complete with teeth and steel blade inserts to make the micro-slots or knifecuts, and fixed in the mould shell in a prearranged irregular order. In some cases the variation in pitch was staggered from rib to rib of the tread design, so that long elements in one rib came alongside those of different length in adjacent rows (Figure 10·5).

In this manner the sound produced by the tyre was changed from

63

a uniform-pitched scream into an un-noticed mutter. The result was obvious to the motorist, and was pointed out to him in a homely simile in which the variable pitch pattern was compared with a line of soldiers crossing a flimsy footbridge and 'breaking step' so that the repeated vibration which would result from marching in step should be avoided. The variable-pitch principle is still in use today.

Two Tier Tread

One other totally different technique, which appeared in the 'thirties, was the two-level 'Duotread' type of pattern, an invention of the Seiberling tyre company of America. The idea, was to make a thick tread, with transverse holes running through from shoulder to shoulder. These holes had two declared purposes. First, they were supposed to pump air through the tread as the tyre rotated, keeping it cool. Second, and more important, when the first tread was worn away, the wear was supposed to break through into the transverse tunnels below and to expose a new simple pattern of transverse grooves and intervening bars. The principle was used under licence by the Avon Company in England. (Figure 10·6)

From limited experience it seems that it was a not particularly effective design. Often the transverse tunnels rendered the tread above them unstable, so that, during the period just before the break-through, the tread wear became irregular. This lumpy wear then persisted as the sub-pattern was revealed, so that it never had a chance to function properly as a second tread.

Inventions galore

The 'thirties continued to be a great time for tyre inventions. The cross-word and the football-pool had not yet captured the imagination of the man in the street, who still had time to brood about the unsatisfactory state of the art of making tyres. Inevitably he produced the same answer to the problems of punctures and skidding many times over. Even today the paper 'Everyday inventions in Tyres and Wheels', written by W. Bond in 1930, often contains the same idea as some inventor of the 'seventies, who has suggested the identical principle all over again.

Many ideas were put forward. Some of them were fundamentally sound but practically impossible. Others were of the type where one asked the inventor: 'What exactly is this supposed to do?', to find so often that he had no idea, but that he thought that it was novel and therefore must be good.

It was left years later, to an automobile engineer, W. R. Boyle of the Rover Company to sum up the whole position:

'Few private inventors have the vaguest idea as to development costs, tooling costs, or production costs. Most of them think that if an idea is sound in principle (many are not even that) it must be capable of successful development and commercially valuable. Nothing can be farther from the truth. To invent an idea which is sound in principle is only a first and elementary step. The really difficult part is the successful solution of all the detail problems and the accurate assessment of costs and commercial possibilities.'

One inventor, who tried a single-handed combat with the established tyre industry, was E. B. Killen, who attempted in the early 'thirties to establish a new range of wide-section low pressure tyres, especially for trucks, to replace the existing high-pressure twin equipment. There was sense in many of his ideas and his claims. But, when brought face to face with an industry which was just beginning to practice some sort of standardisation, of tyre sizes and types, his new and revolutionary ideas, involving a completely new range of tyre sizes, had little chance of making any headway.

E. B. Killen

Although Killen did not have any success during his lifetime, the existence of his patents, including as they did proposals for tyres of tubeless construction in truck sizes, was of the greatest benefit when, years later, companies of world eminence and reputation attempted to establish patent rights to the same basic idea, and found themselves forestalled by the Killen specifications.

In the early 'thirties there was a move, on both sides of the Atlantic to bring the advantages of pneumatic tyres to farming.

Tyres on the Land

So far as Dunlop were concerned the work really began in 1929, with the development of small pneumatic tyres for wheelbarrows, which doubled the load that could be moved over rough ground.

By the early 'thirties the farmer whose land adjoined the Fort Dunlop factory, and one of his friends a few miles away, began to ask about pneumatic tyres for farm carts. The photographs show a comparison between a conventional steel-wheeled farm cart and a modern flat-platform cart with pneumatic tyres (Figure 10·7). The result was an increase in the loads which could be drawn by the horse, of 35-100%, depending on soil conditions.

The range of H.D.V. (horse-drawn-vehicle) or Land tyres was introduced, with suitable axle assemblies and simple brake gear to go with them. They were hailed as a major advance and won medals at the Royal Agricultural show in 1933 and at other shows in Scotland, Ulster and the Irish Free State.

Parallel with these developments, the case of the farm tractor, with its wheels steel straked for grip on the soil, was being considered as a candidate for pneumatic equipment. Early work in America aimed simply at flotation on the soil and used plain treaded aircraft tyres of large section. Dunlop went more seriously into the farm field, using special moulds, with deep tread patterns, to provide grip as well as flotation (Figure 10·8). The spread of the use of the pneumatic tractor tyre was very rapid and the benefits were seen to be so great that the steel straked wheel soon became a thing of the past.

Earthmover tyres

The final stage in the growing up of the pneumatic tyre came with the development of a range of very large scale machinery which could not have been conceived without it. This was the field of large scale earth-handling plant, used for road building, site levelling and airfield construction. Such machinery was first built in the U.S.A., but soon appeared in the United Kingdom, both in imported form and built locally under licence. The provision of tyres required the construction of moulding and tyre building plant, for the making of the new range of very large and ever-increasing low pressure tyres. Low pressure, in this connection, may mean a tyre running at 30-50 lb/sq in, having a sectional width of 21 inches and carrying a load of up to nine tons.

In the years immediately before World War II a shadow aircraft factory was being built on land next-door to Fort Dunlop. The earthmover equipment on the site drew tyre supplies from the factory direct. At one stage, early in production, when outputs were small and constructions somewhat suspect, tyres were being used on the site faster than they could be made.

CHAPTER 11

Tyres and Cornering

A major technical development of the 'thirties was the beginning of an understanding of the part played by the pneumatic tyre in the steering and handling of motor vehicles.

The earliest idea was that which was crystallised by Rudolf Ackermann, who, in 1818 was designing steering systems for horse drawn carriages. He visualised the vehicle cornering about a centre on the line of its rear axle, extended sideways (Figure 11·1). The rear wheels swung round as if the axle was continued and pegged at the centre of the turn. The principle of the steering layout for the front wheels involved the use of a track-rod, with connecting steering arms, which controlled the two wheels. This track-rod was placed behind the front axle and the steering arms were inclined inwards, so that the length of the track-rod was shorter than the distance between the kingpins, about which the wheels steered. In this way, when a turn was made, the two front wheels turned through different angles, the one on the inside of the turn being steered more sharply than that on the outside. Thus a scrubless turn was achieved, with reduced wear on the tyres and less strain on the steering mechanism.

When the automobile arrived, Ackermann's principle was carried over from the horseless carriage as a matter of course. Tyre men were content to leave such things to the vehicle designers. The design was logical and tidy, so what else was there to say? So it came about that the new ideas about the function of pneumatic tyres, in cornering, came, eventually, from outside the tyre industry and mainly from the vehicle makers. These engineers had been conscious for some time

The Ackermann principle

that the actual path of a car in cornering often did not coincide with that laid down by Ackermann.

New investigations

The investigation of what really took place was going on in various parts of the world, quite independently at the end of the 'twenties. In England the National Physical Laboratory had been investigating skidding accidents, on behalf of the Ministry of Transport. Bradley and Allen, who were carrying out the study, used a motorcycle and sidecar as their test vehicle. The sidecar wheel was mounted on a pivot and could be set at an angle to the direction of travel. The resulting forces acting on the wheel could be continuously recorded on a moving paper chart, on a desk built into the front of the sidecar.

The tyre property measured was described as the 'sideways force coefficient.' In the course of carrying out their investigations of dangerous road surfaces, Bradley and Allen became conscious of the fact that the tyre was producing sideways thrusts in the misaligned wheel, without losing its grip on the road.

In the U.S.A. at the same time, K. D. Evans was measuring the cornering properties of tyres, carried on a force-recording frame, running on the drum of a test machine. In France, Broulhiet was carrying out mathematical investigations, supported by road experiments, on the cornering properties of tyres, which he called 'envirage'. In Germany similar work was being done at the Berlin Technical High School.

Cornering force

All these workers came to the same conclusion, in that they saw the pneumatic tyre as cornering by running at a misalignment angle to the direction of travel, and generating a side-thrust or cornering force in the process.

The basic situation is summed up in the two diagrams (Figures 11·2 and 11·3). The first of these, looking at the tyre in plan, shows the vehicle path as the curved dotted line. At any moment we can observe the steered direction, in which the tyre is pointed, and the direction of movement, which is the tangent to the vehicle path at that point. The angle between these two directions is the slip angle, and is a measure of the misalignment at which the tyre runs. Running misaligned in this way, the tyre exerts a push against the road, and it is the reaction of the road to this push which provides the cornering force which eases the vehicle round the corner.

At the same time, the misaligned tyre produces a restoring force, which tends to turn it back into the straight-ahead position, this is shown as the self-aligning torque. In Figure 11·3, we have a plan view of the footprint of contact area of the cornering tyre on the road. As the steered tyre rolls over the road, any point on its centre-line becomes displaced continuously by the sideforce, until the load begins to come off in the last inch or two of the contact. The extent of this displacement is shown by the length of the successive arrows. This explains how the build-up of sideforce takes place progressively, behind the centre of the contact, so that the resulting couple of self-aligning torque is in the direction which tends to unwind the steering and to return it to a straight ahead course.

Neutral-steer

The earliest published work on cornering forces in tyres was set out largely in the form of graphical results, showing the connection between slip angle and the force generated (Figure 11·4).

In the light of this new look at steering and vehicle control, it was necessary to redraw the Ackermann diagram of the car cornering. This now shows (Figure 11·5) the centre of the turn moved forward, ahead of the line of the extension of the back axle, and with the rear tyres as well as the fronts running at slip angles to the direction in which they are pointing. Now all four wheels produce cornering forces, to guide their shares of the weight of the vehicle round the corner.

At first the new insight into the part played by the tyres in car control was publicised in rather obscure terms and there was much confusion and misunderstanding. The first paper to shed real light was that of Maurice Olley, of General Motors in the U.K., who, in 1937, produced some really impressive ideas as to the importance of the part played by tyres in the conditions known as understeer and oversteer. This concept is so important to the better understanding of the relations between tyres and vehicle handling that it will be outlined in detail here.

Consider first of all an elementary car which has equal loads on the front and rear axles and the same tyre pressures all round. At low speeds this car will need equal slip angles at all the four wheels and it will follow the set course held on the steering wheel, round any corner. Such a car is said to be neutral-steered. The conditions under which it is so are critical and will be upset by such alterations of trim or loading as are brought about by the filling and emptying of the fuel tank, the number of passengers in the car, and the amount of luggage in the boot. It follows that neutral-steer conditions are rare and it is more usual to find cars having front and rear loadings which are not equal. The heavier axle then has to produce a larger cornering force, to push itself round the bend, and the wheels on it must therefore run at a larger slip angle than those at the other end of the vehicle.

This means that the car does not follow the set course steered round the corner. The different slip-angles set up, at front and rear, lead it to take a course of its own, and steering corrections have to be made by the driver, once he has set the vehicle on its course round the corner.

Under steer

Two diagrams (Figures 11·6 and 11.7) illustrate this. In the first of these we see the condition where the load on the front axle is larger than that on the rear. Here it is necessary to steer the front wheels into a bigger slip-angle than the rears, to achieve the needed cornering power. The actual path travelled is as shown, with the front wheels taking a wider sweep than those at the rear. It is therefore necessary to add increments of steering as the vehicle runs, so as to hold the car onto the required set course. This condition is appropriately called understeer, and is a very rational situation and easy to cope with, since the extra steering is in the direction of the corner and the whole process comes naturally to all drivers.

Over steer

In the other extreme (Figure 11·7) the rear of the car may be more heavily loaded than the front, for instance with heavy luggage, or with three large passengers in the rear seat. Now we have the opposite situation, where a large slip angle has to be brought into operation, to push the high rear axle weight round the corner. This means that the back of the vehicle 'steps out' on the bend, and the front tends to dive into the direction of the turn, which is taken in a constantly tightening corkscrew. The only hope here, once the car has been steered into the beginning of a turn, is to wind off the steering in the opposite direction, to counteract the direction of the oversteer effect. This is an unnatural operation. It does not come spontaneously to any driver, and if the need to do it is suddenly encountered, the average motorist will probably make a mess of it. Furthermore it must be realised that, in practice, we are faced with a situation where the correction of oversteer on the first steering effort will be followed by a similar oversteered swing in the opposite direction, which may itself go out of control, and in default of a second correction may lead to the loss of control of the car.

All these ideas were formulated during the 'thirties, at a time when there was a growing collaboration between the tyre technician and the vehicle design engineer. Much of the early writing about the effects was confused and difficult to grasp and to apply. During the years of relative inactivity in the European vehicle industry, during World War II, the ideas were digested and became better understood, with the result that the industry expanded again after the war with a considerable advance in comprehension of the part played by tyres in vehicle handling.

At Fort Dunlop the problem was studied by J. H. Hardman, and was summed up in his paper 'Tyres and Steering', published by the "Institute of Road Transport Engineers" in 1949. Hardman's investigation, carried out largely on the floor of the basement of a large building, showed that understeer and oversteer could be detected as a growing or a shrinking of the turning circle, even when the car was pushed round by hand, at 1 m.p.h., with the steering locked.

Today, this matter of the relation of tyre slip angles, front and rear, to vehicle handling and behaviour, is well understood. Family cars are designed to be slightly understeered, in their normal condition of load. This means that handling falls naturally into the pattern which is understood by their users.

Adjustments may be made, where necessary, to the steering properties of a given model by alterations in the relative inflation pressures of front and rear tyres. The aim, for understeer and stability, is that the front tyres must run at a slightly larger slip angle than the rear tyres. With some rear-engined cars, this means that there may have to be large differences in inflation pressures between front and rear tyres. For instance, the Hillman 'Imp', in spite of its aluminium cylinder block, needed tyre pressures of 15 lb/sq. in. in front tyres with 30 lb/sq. in. in the rear ones.

Tyres and steering

CHAPTER 12

World War II

For the six years of World War II development work on the car tyre ceased. Of necessity output was limited to keeping the wheels of essential transport moving while the product itself was very considerably degraded to reduce rubber consumption.

Truck tyres and aviation tyres were a different matter. There had to be large production, in special patterns and in a number of sizes, for the armed service vehicles. In military aviation the coming of hard concrete runways led to a change-over to tyres of smaller section running at higher inflation pressures.

A booklet, produced by the Tyre Manufacturers' Conference in 1946, 'Tyres and the War', gave the total score of vehicle tyres made in Britain during the war as 32.7 million, together with 47 million cycle tyres. Below are a few of the main features of this wartime activity.

Truck tyre patterns

In the years just before the war a cross-country truck tyre had been developed, for use on army vehicles and other transport. The tread design consisted of heavy traction bars. Initially these were arranged, on the tread surface, in a helical bar configuration (Figure 12·1). Although the grip potential kept the tyre driving on loose surfaces, the natural reaction was for the tyre to edge sideways as much as forwards. This not very satisfactory tendency was reduced by adding a solid central stop-rib, down the centreline of the tread, at the mould closure (Figure 12·2). Even so the design remained somewhat suspect on loose or muddy terrain. For use on snow in the Alps the Swiss Post Office used right and left-handed tyres fitted on the opposite sides of the vehicles, to neutralise the sideways movement. Later designs used a balanced arrangement of bars so that the sideways effort was cut out inside the pattern itself (Figure 12·3).

Puncture resistance

Work was also undertaken for the War Office on the puncture proofing of tyres for army transport. The earliest idea put forward

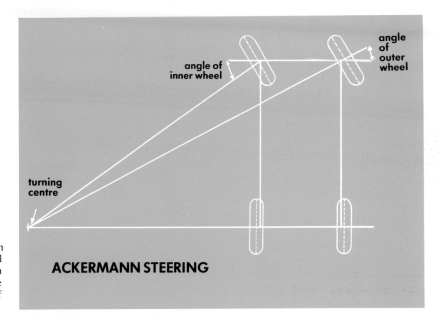

ACKERMANN STEERING

angle of outer wheel

angle of inner wheel

turning centre

Figure 11.1
The basic idea behind the Ackermann steering principle. The inner wheel turns through a greater angle than the outer wheel and the vehicle turns about a point on the line of the rear axle.

Figure 11.2
Plan view of tyre cornering. The slip angle is measured between the steered direction and the tangent to the curved path.

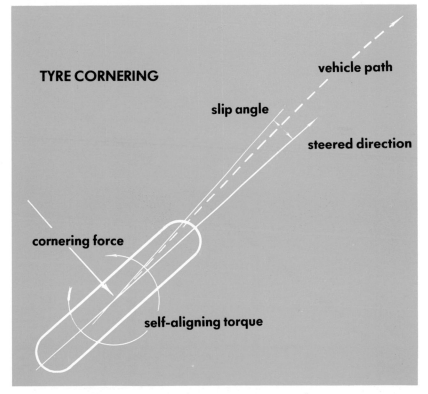

TYRE CORNERING

vehicle path

slip angle

steered direction

cornering force

self-aligning torque

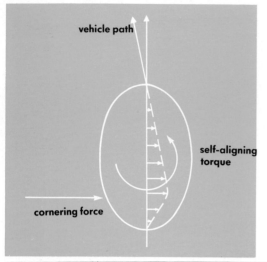

vehicle path

self-aligning
torque

cornering force

Figure 11.3
Footprint of tyre when cornering,
showing build-up of the side-force
progressively behind the centre of
contact, producing a self-aligning
torque tending to straighten out the
steering.

Figure 11.4
Cornering force graph for a typical
medium-size car tyre. A sideways
force of 200lb. is produced at a slip
angle of 2½°.

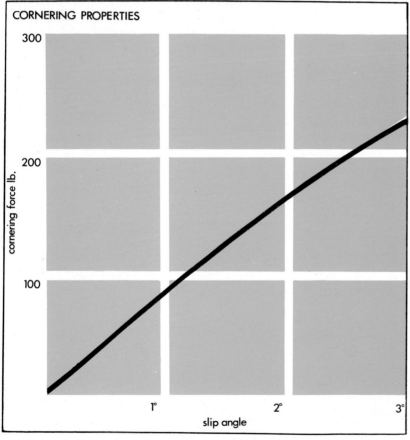

CORNERING PROPERTIES

300

200

100

cornering force lb.

1°   2°   3°

slip angle

Figure 11.5
A car cornering. The centre of the turn is ahead of the line of the rear axle and all tyres are running at slip angles to produce the cornering efforts needed to push their share of the vehicles weight round the corner.

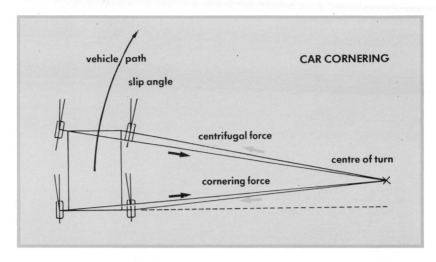

Figure 11.6
The stable understeer condition, where the slip angles, at which the tyres set themselves to produce the required cornering power are larger at the front wheels than at the rears. As the car corners, extra small steering efforts, in the same direction are needed to keep the car on course.

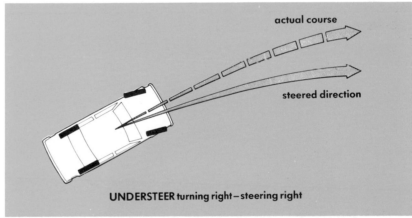

Figure 11.7
The oversteer condition, where the slip angle required to produce the needed cornering force at the rear axle is greater than that required at the front wheels. The car is very unstable and tends to go into a spiral path, unless 'opposite lock' is applied.

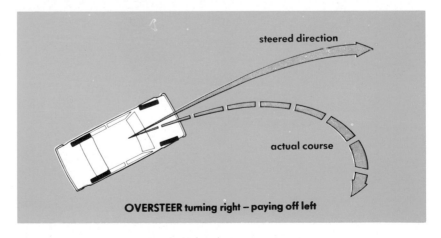

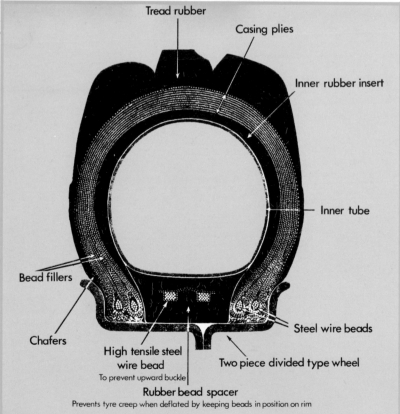

Tread rubber

Casing plies

Inner rubber insert

Inner tube

Bead fillers

Chafers

High tensile steel
wire bead
To prevent upward buckle

Rubber bead spacer
Prevents tyre creep when deflated by keeping beads in position on rim

Steel wire beads

Two piece divided type wheel

Figure 12.1, top left.
Cross country or snow tyre pattern, with helical bar tread, producing side thrusts as well as traction.

Figure 12.2, top centre.
Centre stop-rib added to prevent side thrust.

Figure 12.3, top right.
Balanced pattern giving forward travel without side thrust.

Figure 12.4.
The Run-flat tyre, used normally inflated, but capable of limited running after having been punctured by gunfire or other damage.

was for what was called a pneumatic tyre support. Here the compressed air in the tyre was completely replaced by a rubber annulus, with moulded internal voids within it. The device carried the load and made the tyre independent of inflation pressure. The P.T. support was very heavy and expensive, fitting of tyre to wheel was accomplished only with the aid of a hydraulic press and the performance of the tyre was limited.

The P.T. support was therefore replaced by a new type of tyre which ran as a conventional inflated pneumatic tyre, under all normal conditions. Construction included a thick rubber lining, inside the walls, thinning out towards the crown. If this tyre was punctured, so that the air escaped, then the reinforced walls were capable of carrying the load of the truck and allowing the vehicle to return to base under its own power. This met the original specification and it was soon found that vehicles fitted with the new tyre did not have to return to base but could safely complete their mission first.

Here is a quote from a cable received by the War Office from the battlefield: '*Cars equipped R.F. tyres engaged in raid on enemy lines of communication. Subjected three hours concentrated air attack. Three cars set alight, one knocked out gunfire, remaining three cars with all tyres punctured covered seventy miles by night to own lines. Commanding Officer reports that but for R.F. tyres entire squadron would have been lost.*'

A section of the Run Flat tyre is illustrated (Figure 12·4). Note the thick load-bearing rubber lining, and the use of a bead-spacer to hold the edges of the cover securely in place on the rim when running without air pressure. This general assembly was based on practice which had been worked out as a safety measure on tyres for the World's speed record, at speeds in the 200-300 m.p.h. bracket.

R.F. tyres

When America came into the war, late in 1941, the design was made available to our Allies. As made in the U.S.A. the tyre was renamed the Combat tyre, the main change in the layout being to redesign the heavy and expensive bead spacer, which became a spider device made of welded steel strip. The modification of the assembly was the subject of an American Patent and an attempt was made to sell the rights in it back to Britain—an amusing ploy.

Combat tyres

As a result of excellent and painstaking liaison between the War Office and the British tyre industry, in the years leading up to World

73

War II, the general level of equipment fitted to British trucks was very high. A captured order from Rommel to his commanders in the Western Desert emphasised this. It was dated 15 December 1941, and read: '*For the reconnaisance, as indeed for every desert reconnaisance, only captured English trucks are to be used since German trucks stick in the sand too often.*'

The main reason for such supremacy was the selection of low pressure tyres, of adequate sectional width, so that they could be run at really low pressures when necessary.

This army experience contrasted strangely with the general practice in Europe and the Near East, in the period just before the War. There was a general move to change over truck tyres to low pressure ranges with larger sections. Vehicle licensing laws, however, favoured high pressure tyres, and although dual marked tyres, for instance 34 x 7 7.50-20, were available, they were almost always used as the high pressure version and had to be strong enough to stand up to use in that way.

Thus the European tyre was tougher, and of course more expensive to make, than the new standard low-pressure range which was coming into use in the U.S.A. The contrast was well illustrated, in the latter stages of the war, when Tyre Control received orders for 34 x 7 tyres for use on civil transport in the Near East. Supplies of the American dual-marked range were used to fill the gap. These tyres failed completely to produce the 34 x 7 performance which had been required, but which had never been designed into them in their U.S.A. factories.

The coming of synthetic rubber

In December 1941 the Japanese struck at the U.S.A. fleet at Pearl Harbour, and the two nations were at war. The subsequent over-running of Malaya and the Dutch East Indies, completed by midsummer of 1942, deprived the Western allies of their major source of natural rubber. Of the areas where first-quality plantation rubber was produced, only Ceylon (Sri Lanka) remained in allied hands. All the rest was lost by conquest in those few months.

The Tyre Manufacturers' Conference, in Great Britain, set up a Technical Committee, first to conserve the stockpile of natural rubber which remained, and subsequently to help in the introduction of synthetic substitutes for natural rubber, as they became available.

The industry set itself a programme, reserving the stocks of natural rubber for use in tyres where it was indispensable, e.g. in aeroplane and large truck covers, and at the same time reducing, in a series of controlled steps, the amount of natural rubber in car, cycle and other less-stressed tyres.

It should be recalled that the supply of rubber from Ceylon, which was still in British hands, would have been sufficient to cover all our needs of rubber. If we had been able to retain this output for our own use, we need not have been troubled by major conservation measures or by the introduction of synthetic rubber into our tyre production. The collaboration between the western allies was, however, very intimate and under the stress of the times very rapid in action. The Ceylon output was therefore placed at the disposal of the allies and, inevitably, the major part of it went to the American manufacturers who had the same problem with the making of cool-running aeroplane and large truck and earthmover tyres, which was possible only with the use of natural rubber compounds.

The story of the production of large quantities of synthetic rubber, in a very short time, need not be told in detail here. It was decided that the work should be carried out in the relative safety of the U.S.A. and Canada, rather than by transporting the basic raw materials to this air-raid ridden country, across the submarine-infested oceans.

The process, based on the building of the large rubber molecule from simpler ones, is known as polymerisation of monomers. It had been practiced, in a crude form, by the Germans, in the First World War. Now it was carried out with much greater precision, with the materials in emulsion form. (The process was based on a co-poly-merisation, primarily of butadiene, which has the characteristic diene double-bond structure found in rubber, the molecule being loaded up by inclusion of the ring-form styrene molecule.)

As soon as a satisfactory polymer had been arrived at, the process was standardised, for the duration of the war, and the plants which had been built in the U.S.A. and Canada went rapidly into production. The material was at first known as GR-S, standing for Government Rubber-Styrene type.

GR-S

Trial quantities of GR-S were available for manufacturing trials in the United Kingdom by late 1942 and full production quantities were coming in by mid 1943. Whatever the harrassed technicians may have thought about the material at the time, this was a major war-winning achievement by the American petro-chemical industry, and calls for the greatest acclamation.

So far as being a true replacement for natural rubber the new material had many shortcomings. It was not as tacky in its unvulcanised form, and tyre building was slower and needed assistance from solutions at tread joints and similar areas of stress. It needed more mill power to masticate and mix. On the tyre, the resulting tread ran hotter than natural rubber setting the limitations on its use which have already been mentioned. It was satisfactory for the car tyres of wartime standard manufacture, although the wartime motorist was aware that something had changed, when he found that he could no longer manhandle his vehicle in and out of the garage, due to extra tyre drag. It could be used in small truck tyres and in the small proportions in which any form of new rubber hydrocarbon was allowed in cycle tyres.

Problems of synthetics

But, so far as the more arduous uses were concerned, synthetic rubber was not good enough. These applications included tyres for aeroplanes, large trucks and earthmovers, heavy fast cars, and the solid tyres used on fast moving armoured vehicles, for track support and guidance.

By the end of the war, in the summer of 1945, the North American synthetic rubber industry was producing at a rate equal to a million tons a year. The rate was cut back when the war ended, so that a million tons was not produced again for several years. But that is the record of the industry, which, starting from various sources, as different as petroleum residues, molasses, potatoes and maize, produced a completely uniform standard product in vast quantities.

The story of what happened after the war will be told later. For the present it is enough to say that the synthetic material, which was introduced as a wartime life-saver, was not dropped afterwards, as we all prayed that it might be when it first appeared. By virtue of its own special properties, at first unsuspected, and with a new realisation of the effect of compound properties on tyre performance it was seen to enable a new kind of improved tyre to be made.

Inner tubes

The plan, as far as tubes were concerned, was to have a separate synthetic rubber, known as 'butyl' for their manufacture. This material, GR-I, or Government Rubber Isobutylene-type, had greatly enhanced resistance to permeability or diffusion of air. But here the programme ran late, due to the fact that the provision of the required isobutylene raw material, in quantity, cut across the high-octane fuel requirements of the U.S.A. and other airforces. In consequence GR-S was, for a time, used for making tubes. It was a poor substitute.

76

The material was satisfactory for tyre treads, but when made into a thin tube and subjected to inflation stretch, it suffered from its poor resistance to tear. GR-S truck tubes were the first products that the writer heard described, by a visiting American Army supply officer, as 'a product of minimum adequacy'!

The other great revolution, brought about by the Second World War, was the replacement of cotton by rayon and nylon, in the textile casings of tyres. Up to the beginning of the war, interest in rayon had been very tentative. Cotton, mainly from Egypt, had been the textile material used for all tyre casings, with the very small exception of the silk used in tubular cycle race tyres.

Tyre companies had cotton mills, linked in with their organisations, staffed by experts who understood the particular problems of spinning and doubling cotton, to produce tyre cords with the required properties, and at an economic price.

In the years immediately before the Second World War, there had been a few tentative experiments in the use of rayon in tyres. There were difficulties here, which offset the obvious strength advantages of the rayon (artificial silk) cord, which was made up of long continuous extruded filaments, instead of the mass of relatively short length hairs, which made up a cotton cord.

The cotton cord stuck easily to natural rubber, and the surface of the cord, with its protruding fibre ends, entangled easily with the film of rubber which was rolled or ground onto it. In contrast, rayon cord had a bright lustrous surface, made up of shiny continuous filaments, to which rubber did not adhere in a satisfactory manner. It was therefore necessary to treat the surface of the cord with a dip, consisting usually of rubber latex, formaldehyde and resorcinol, to enable the rubber to bond onto it.

In the late 'thirties rayon truck tyres, made by the technique just described, were tried out in small numbers. They were used, for example, on the trucks used in East Anglia for the collection of the sugar-beet harvest and its transport to factories. This is heavy short-term work, operating over rough tracks and with some inevitable overloading. The cotton tyre of the day suffered from impact fractures, due to sheer abuse, and from casing breakup due to the overloading. The advent of the experimental rayon tyres gave immediate signs of improvement in performance and a reduction of dramatic proportions, in the scale of failures experienced. Small

Synthetic textiles

Rayon

77

numbers of these rayon tyres were sent to selected overseas markets, where conditions were especially severe.

The introduction of rayon as a general material for tyre casings came about during the period of rubber conservation from 1943 onwards. The change was made from cotton to rayon not, as in the pre-war experiments, with the object of making stronger tyres, but as a rubber-saving measure. Rayon enabled a tyre of a given strength to be made thinner than was possible in cotton, and this thinner casing needed less of the precious stocks of rubber, to insulate ply from ply.

Introduced in this way, the techniques required for the use of rayon in tyre casings became established in the small-scale production of car and truck tyres which was involved under wartime conditions. When the expansion of the industry began again, after the war, rayon was established and all the know-how for its use was worked out, so that cotton never reappeared in the car and truck tyre ranges.

Nylon

The introduction of nylon was also a wartime change. This material, developed by W. H. Carothers in the U.S.A., provided the new, highly stretchy, filaments which were used for purposes ranging from glamour hosiery of unbelievable endurance to glider tow-ropes of high snatch resistance. So far as tyres were concerned, nylon offered opportunities to build light weight casings of great strength and impact resistance. Such casings were first seen in this country in tyres on military aircraft, operated by the United States Air Force. To those of us who were keeping the score on aircraft tyre performance the effect of these new tyres was surprising. So great was the increase in strength and resistance to impact, with the new material, that impact fractures, which had been the chief cause of premature tyre removal, practically disappeared from the records.

Aircraft practice

The fact that nylon soon completely replaced earlier casing materials in aeroplane tyres was not, however, just on the basis of increased resistance to impact and abuse. As the war ended and commercial aviation opened up, the era of the concrete surfaced runways was established, so that the large section tyres used on grass were replaced by the smaller high-pressure equipment.

The availability of a stronger casing material was seized on by the aircraft designer, as a means of obtaining a small-section tyre, of lighter weight, to carry the same load as the earlier rayon tyre. Once ranges of nylon tyres had been established on this basis, there was no more scope for the rather heavier rayon equipment, and it consequently disappeared.

This point underlines the fact that the aircraft designer regards his landing gear as a cumbersome means of getting the aircraft into the air and returning it to the ground. In flight the tyres are unwanted volume and weight. Anything that can be done to reduce wheel and tyre size eases the problem of stowage and increases payload.

As the tyre equipment of aircraft changed over from low pressure tyres some of the earlier practices were left behind. For instance, the low pressure tyre had often been carried on a neat cast aluminium or magnesium wheel, which had a rim supporting the tyre on the outside and carrying the steel brake-drum within, fixed directly to its inner surface. Although the layout was economical in space, always of prime importance in aircraft practice, it introduced the old problem of brake heat affecting the tyre beads, the tube and its valve. When the new equipment, for the high pressure range was designed the brake drum was separated from the rim base and adequate cooling assured.

A similar point applies to the earthmover tyre range. Here is a tyre which, in the course of its work, suffers continuous hard shocks and has to resist the effects of this hammering while running at a fair speed and at intermittent high loads. Again the introduction of nylon into earthmover and similar high load tyres, towards the end of World War II, produced a dramatic reduction in the proportion of tyres ruined by impact bursts. This advantage made itself felt over the succeeding decade, until nylon became accepted as the standard material for earthmover tyre construction, to the exclusion of rayon.

The spread of the use of nylon to car and truck tyres, and to tyres for the special purposes of racing, came in the decade after the war.

CHAPTER 13

No Tube
– No Trouble

The automobile industry of Western Europe came out of the war and spent the last years of the 'forties reorganising itself, turning from the production of specialised machines, with which the war had been won, to the competitive cars and commercial vehicles of peace.

So far as tyres were concerned the use of rayon for casings remained from wartime practice in both the U.S.A. and Western Europe, and nylon came progressively into use where it had advantages.

The industry in Britain was re-established largely on natural rubber, eked out by a continuation of the wartime use of reclaim and rubber crumb. Synthetic rubber was no longer freely available, as it now became a dollar import from North America and currency was not made available for this purpose until the 'fifties.

America, on the other hand, turned over its vast industry to peacetime commercial purposes under conditions where prudence demanded that the synthetic industry must be kept in being. It was however throttled back to just over half its capacity at the end of the war; an output which had to be absorbed by the tyre industry, willy-nilly.

Circumstances therefore required that the post-war American car tyre was still made entirely from synthetic rubber. But the material used was not the same as that which had kept the wheels turning during the latter years of the conflict. Those wartime tyres had not been of very high quality and there were many recollections of disappointment with their performance.

'Cold Rubber'

So it came about that the synthetic rubber factories, when the standard wartime process came to be relaxed, introduced a new and

80

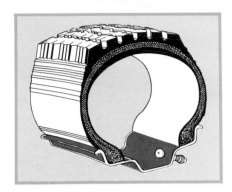

Figure 13.1
Early form of tubeless tyre with plastic self-sealing layer on the inner surface casing.

Figure 13.2
Granite sett road from Liverpool, relaid as part of the Fort Dunlop tyre proving ground.

Figure 13.3
Dunlop D2/103 pattern, with high concentration of knife slots in the tread.

Figure 13.4, far right
Dunlop WH2 pattern, with wet-hold improved by very high concentration of knife slots in the tread.

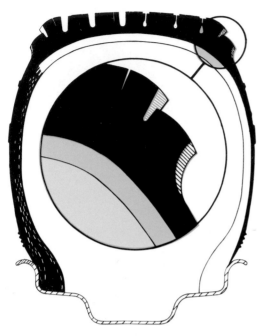

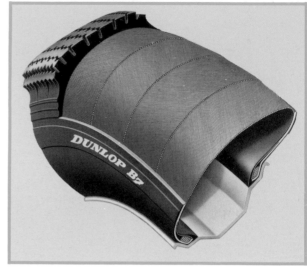

Figure 13.5, top left.
The safety shoulder, first used in Dunlop tyres in Germany and subsequently adopted by designers of cross-ply tyres world wide. The feature enables longitudinal lines and joints in the road surface to be crossed without the steering of the car being disturbed.

Figure 13.6, top right.
The Dunlop Germany 'B7' tyre with the safety shoulder.

Figure 13.8, below right.
The introduction of high grip treads on motorcycle race tyres made it possible to pick out riders using them by the greater angles of lean which could be achieved, and the consequently greater cornering speed. The rider on the right is using the new tyre.

Figure 13.7
The difference between an ordinary tyre, left, and the tyre with the safety shoulder, right, when crossing a raised line on the road surface.

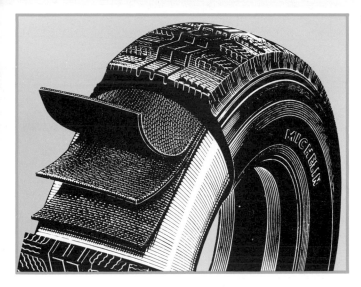

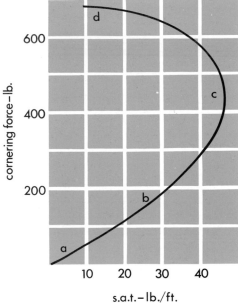

GOUGH PLOT 6·70–15 24p.s.i. 1100 lb.

cornering force–lb.

s.a.t.–lb./ft.

Figure 13.9, above right
The Gough Plot showing the relation between self-aligning-torque, or feel-at-the-wheel, and the cornering force produced by the tyre as slip-angle is increased.

Figure 13.10, above
Michelin's original diagram of the construction of the steel-braced 'X' radial-ply car tyre.

Figure 13.11, right
Pirelli's early 'Cinturato' radial tyre with textile-belted tread.

Figure 13.12, far right
Dunlop Germany's 'SP3' textile-braced tyre with dog-bone tread design.

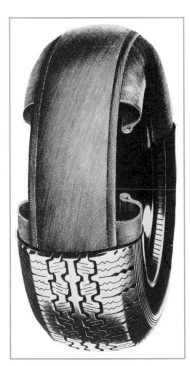

Figure 13.13, left.
The Roadtrak RK8 tyre, for specialised off-the-road work such as quarrying, combining good grip and resistance to damage.

Figure 13.14, below.
The Roadtrak RK9 tyre, capable of use on hard roads without producing irregular wear and giving good traction when used on building sites for collection and delivery of loads.

improved form of rubber polymer. 'Synthetic' had a bad reputation. The new material, although of the same type and lineage, was not called synthetic at all. Taking the cue from the fact that the improved properties of the new material came from polymerising it at a lower temperature than previously practised, the new product was launched as 'cold rubber'. Much publicity was given to it; the industry's suppliers of compounding ingredients devised special additives to suit it; and very good tyres were built from it.

These new improved rubber polymers were made available to Europe and were gratefully accepted and incorporated into the programme of improvements in tyre grip. They also provided knowledge which was invaluable to the synthetic rubber factory, which was eventually set up on a co-operative basis by the British rubber industry, at Fawley, in Hampshire, in 1957.

Immediately after the war there was considerable experiment in the U.S.A. directed to the revival of the tubeless tyre, in a form suitable for modern motor cars. The designs which had been used in cycle tyres, forty years earlier, were reappraised. What was now sought was the avoidance of sudden deflation followed by possible loss of vehicle control, due to the tearing of a stretched inner tube when punctured. Dispensing with the tube made it possible to experiment with plastic layers, on the inner surface of the casing, to seal up nail punctures as they arose and so eliminate delays on the road (Figure 13·1).

Tubeless tyres

Such tyres appeared on the replacement market, both in America and in the United Kingdom. Dunlop sponsored an observed test by the R.A.C., in which a car was fitted with tyres of this type, which were ceremoniously punctured by having a number of nails driven into them. The car was then driven to Fort William and back to London, without loss of pressure or any other incident.

By 1954, enough experience had been obtained, both in manufacture and performance of tubeless tyres, to make it clear that a simple form of construction, without the sealant layer, would have advantages in service, being able to "convert the blow-out into a slow-out", —as the publicity writers put it. The result of puncturing a tubeless tyre was that it generally went flat slowly, overnight, in the garage, rather than deflating rapidly on the road. Experience, based on the observation of hundreds of tyres, showed that the number of punctures causing road delays was extended from an average of one in 16,000 miles, on tubed tyres, to something like one in 80,000 miles on tubeless equipment.

Car design engineers asked for reassurance about the performance of tubeless tyres under various conditions of normal abuse. Dunlop's young engineer, Gordon Shearer, investigated all these problems and produced filmed records of the tests that were carried out. As 'No Tube — No Trouble' this film was widely shown on technical college courses for motorists and to clubs. A copy was also requested for preservation in the National Film Archive.

The tubeless tyre had a further practical advantage of interest to the car manufacturer, in that it could be fitted and inflated, by automatic means, on the production line.

Dunlop, with their then very large share of the supply of original equipment tyres for British cars, were the first to introduce the tubeless tyre in this country. The industry changed over rapidly to the new kind of equipment and the tubeless tyre was soon accepted by motorists as the norm.

Wet Grip

During the 'fifties great strides were made in the United Kingdom in understanding the way in which tyres grip wet roads. This constituted a contribution to road safety of the first order, and as such it merits study in some detail.

The major contributions to the solution of the problem came from Dunlop, and from other manufacturers who had contracts to supply the car makers. Inevitably the work was concentrated on the problems of the high speed car, but there were developments in other tyre fields as a result.

Early in the 'fifties car engineers began to complain to visiting tyre engineers that tyres currently available suffered from loss of grip at high speed in the wet. The phenomenon was described in emotional terms, as 'lightening off', 'going light in the wet' and similar expressions. Experiments were made to investigate these claims, and a one week-old car was completely burnt out in the process. It was replaced within a week, which speaks as much for the seriousness of the problem as for the determination with which it was being tackled.

It was soon established that high speed testing was not necessary, and that the problem could be worked out under controlled conditions at moderate speeds. The investigation moved to some polished granite sett roads in the dock area of Liverpool, working early on Sunday mornings with the fire brigade in attendance to hose down the road. Subsequently a stretch of Garston High Street, in Liverpool, was found to be due for relaying, and the polished setts from this surface were bought and laid as part of a new proving ground at Fort Dunlop (Figure 13·2).

Interest in wet grip was intense, and the car design engineers were insistent that tyre performance in this direction had to be improved. The British tyre industry owed much to these promptings from the car designers; their demands provided the irritant which led to the carrying out of simple programmes of work that led fairly quickly to a new generation of tyres with a great increase in safety.

The first attack was through the medium of tread pattern. The way was fairly clearly seen, as the development of a ribbed pattern, with a higher concentration of knifeslots in the tread surface had been proceeding for a long period. An example, dated 1956-57 is shown in (Figure 13·3).

Various designs, with an even higher concentration of slots in the tread, were prepared at Fort Dunlop, and tested carefully on the wet pave and other surfaces. The choice fell on a pattern coded 'WH.2' (W.H. = wet hold) (Figure 13·4). This tyre was sent to the more vociferous of the car engineers. The acceptance was favourable and there followed one of those quiet periods, so far as Dunlop were concerned, during which it was imagined that the new tyre was being used as a goad to spur on other tyre manufacturers to efforts along similar lines.

Also in the 'fifties a separate problem was being worked on in Germany. This was described in various terms, as wander, white line sensitivity, or ridging.

Wander

The symptoms are simply set down: The disturbing feature is any longitudinal edge or obstruction, running along the surface of the road. In Germany, the most prevalent source of trouble was the road paved with blue basalt setts, presenting a continuous pattern of longitudinal edges disposed along the road.

In other places the longitudinal edge was produced on the road by the 'white lines', dividing the carriageway into lanes. These are usually marked with a plastic paint, applied hot to the road surface. After two or three repaintings the line could stand proud of the surrounding surface by 1/8 to 1/4 inch. Alternatively, in areas where roads were built in large panels of concrete, the longitudinal feature was formed by a centre joint between the panels, often running for miles continuously down the centre of the road. This joint was usually filled with bitumen, to seal the gap and to enable expansion and contraction of the panels to take place in hot and cold weather.

The effect of such longitudinal features in the road surface on the handling of the car was often disturbing; especially when an overtaking manoeuvre was attempted. This usually involved crossing the centreline of the road and returning again to the nearside after the other vehicle had been passed. The longitudinal line on the road produced a hesitation when crossed in both directions. Instead of a normal sinuous movement, from lock to lock, there were two obstructive lurches in the transition, as the edge of the tyre sidewall caught against the raised obstruction on the road.

It was recognised as the old problem that occurred with bicycle tyres in the tramlines, and the Trojan car, with its solid tyres, which, being similarly trapped, had to go all the way to the tram depot!

At speeds around 20-30 m.p.h. the difficulty produced was slight. At twice that speed, or more, the disturbance of the planned overtaking manoeuvre was much more dramatic and there were chances of the raised line on the road taking charge of the steering of the car, and leading to an accident.

Experimental work carried out on this problem by Dunlop in Germany, resulted in the design of a tyre with two small extra ribs added to the edges of the tread and stepped down slightly from the normal level of the pattern (Figure 13·5). This was called the Sicherheit Schulter (safety shoulder), and was incorporated in the 'B7' pattern which Deutsche Gummi Dunlop introduced in 1959 (Figure 13·6).

The safety shoulder worked caterpillar-fashion, as the tyre encountered a raised ridge on the road. The tyre was led up the step through the intermediary of the safety shoulder, which climbed up first, followed by the tread-edge, without any tangling of the tyre edge against the ridge. This feature was a satisfactory solution to the problem and was readily accepted. An illustration from the original German publicity shows the difference in car reaction with and without the safety shoulder (Figure 13·7). In spite of intensive patent cover the safety shoulder was widely copied in Europe and there is a report of it being shown at a conference of American tyre manufacturers as the latest development by their German organisation.

Some manufacturers used a less effective design in which the tread was extended in a clean sweep round and onto the upper wall. This was the wrap-around tread. Both design features became an important part of the design of cross-ply covers and were forsaken only when radial tyres took over. The radial belted tread had its built-in caterpillar device, which led it safely over road ridges without entanglement.

In the late 'fifties there was interest in the U.S.A. and elsewhere in high grip treads. There had been an attempt to popularise the use of butyl rubber for use in tyre treads and casings. At first this was done as an experiment by the oil companies, as major producers of synthetic rubber, to determine if it would be possible to move the Tyre Industry to the use of only one synthetic rubber instead of two.

High grip tread

While butyl had obvious merits as the polymer for the air retaining inner liner of tubeless tyres, it was incompatible with GR-S and with natural rubber, so that the whole tyre structure had to be changed over to its use. This attack on the Tyre Industry did not succeed, but the protagonists of butyl tyres found that they had an unsuspected good feature at their command. The dead butyl tread was found to have a greatly improved grip on the road than the earlier livelier compounds of GR-S or natural rubber.

The line of attack was therefore turned in this direction and butyl covers were marketed in the U.S.A. as a special safety tyre. Fairly large quantities were made for experimental trial in the United Kingdom. The dangers of getting butyl mixed with normal tyre compounds, with complete loss of all adhesion between the affected parts of the tyre structure, were avoided by confining manufacture to one factory and doing the work at weekends under strictly supervised conditions.

It was soon realised that the properties which gave butyl treads a high road grip could be matched by a suitably modified form of GR-S, with higher styrene content. This material was made first in Dunlop's pilot polymer plant, at Fort Dunlop, and subsequently handed over to the new International Synthetic Rubber factory, at Fawley, who made it for all their customers as a routine polymer.

One of the earliest uses of the new tread was in motorcycle race tyres. Here it was an immediate success. In photographs appearing in the press it was possible to pick out the men with the high-grip treads, by the greater angle of lean which they could safely achieve when cornering (Figure 13·8).

The 'fifties saw one more development in the science of cornering, which was outlined in Chapter 11. Eric Gough, working at Fort Dunlop, realised the difficulty of making use of the information on the properties of a tyre, as shown in the usual standard graph of its cornering force. This showed the force generated at various slip angles (Figure 13·9). It was meaningless to the motorist, who could never see his tyres when he was cornering and had no idea of the direction in which they were pointing at any particular time.

The Gough Plot

Gough pointed out that it would be much more helpful if the cornering force were plotted against the self-aligning force, which was a feature of the steering situation that the driver could feel for himself as the reaction at the steering wheel. The resulting graph soon became linked with his name internationally, as the Gough Plot (Figure 13·10). It enables the steering properties of any tyre to be stated concisely and to be read off easily by anyone interested. Thus the parts of the plot may be summed up as follows:

Lower part of the curve, a—b.

The cornering force increases proportionately to the reaction on the wheel. This is the area of the curve which is used by the ordinary motorist.

Middle of the curve, b—c.

The cornering force continues to increase, but the growth of the reaction at the wheel begins to slow down. This is the area of the curve which is used by the skilful sports car driver.

Top of the curve, c—d.

The cornering force is still increasing slowly, but the reaction at the steering wheel is now falling rapidly. This is the area of racing tyre operation and is explored only by brave men.

Dr Gough, as he became in 1966, contributed this very useful method of describing the cornering properties of tyres and it has become established as a new standard of technical description.

Radial ply tyres

At the end of World War II a new development in tyre construction came into being. Michelin in France were faced with a wear problem on the heavy front-wheel drive Citroen cars. The solution to the problem is of great interest as an example of the use of mathematical argument, in isolation, to produce a product with new properties.

The logic of the case is simple. The problem is to make a tyre which will last twice as long as any construction yet produced. Now tyres wear out because they have to run misaligned, (to produce the cornering force to push the vehicle round the corners). So, if we make a tyre which produces its cornering power at a smaller misalignment, or slip angle, then it should wear slower.

That this was, in fact, the train of thought behind the Michelin work is shown in the key words of the patent filed in France in June 1946, and which was translated into English a year later: '. . . . . *an outer cover which will give increased resistance to wear. . . . .*'

The construction used was highly original, the operative part being a structure, immediately below the tread, consisting of layers of steel cord, built up as a rigid band. In order that this structure might have the maximum effect in guiding the tread of the tyre, so that it functioned as a rigid hoop, the casing below was made flexible, by building it of radial cords of rayon, which ran directly from bead to bead as horseshoe-like loops, at right angles to the circumference of the tyre (Figure 13·10). Such tyres are commonly called after the radial casing, but it is the rigid-breaker structure which gives them their long wearing properties.

Michelin were in a good position to make a success of this new construction, especially as they already had considerable experience in the use of steel cord in tyres. They had been making truck-tyres, of conventional cross-ply construction, with casings made from steel cable, the kind of construction which had been used for many years in cable controls known as Bowden cable. Michelin had spent much effort on making a cable of this type with steel of rigidly controlled properties and constructional features which made it suitable for use in the special conditions existing within a running tyre.

It is interesting to note that a construction of this type, with a rigid steel reinforced tread band called a 'girder-belt', carried on a radial casing, was patented as early as 1913 in England, by Gray and Sloper. In the absence of the necessary techniques which were needed to bond such a composite structure of rubber and steel together, the invention was never exploited. It is doubtful, in any case, if the inventors really saw clearly what they were trying to achieve, and even more certain that the rubber compounds of those times would have failed to produce the possible mileage potential.

The new tyre, the Michelin 'X', was tested and was found to last about twice as long as the conventional cross-ply cover. At this stage it was launched on the market in car tyre sizes, reaching England in 1953. Reaction was mixed. The mileage increase was there, and the tyre was being used on a wide scale in France, where its economy made it acceptable on the small French family cars, no matter what its other properties might be.

But the major alteration in its slip-angle properties produced important reactions elsewhere, which made the new tyre questionable for use on many cars. This position has changed in the subsequent years, and radials have been established as the construction of the future.

The outstanding change in the handling of cars fitted with 'X' tyres was a sensation of 'running on rails'. This encouraged cornering at high speeds, with a feeling of great safety. Unfortunately the tyre gave no progressive warning that breakaway was about to take place and, until motorists with high performance cars became accustomed to the new tyres, there was a liability to occasional violent breakaway when cornering adhesion limits were inadvertently exceeded.

Full acceptance of the new tyre had to wait for new cars to be designed around it, beginning with the Citroen 'DS' model with its oleo-pneumatic suspension, introduced in 1955-6, and followed by similar vehicles of less revolutionary design from Peugeot.

So far as the rest of the tyre makers of Europe were concerned, Michelin's tight patent coverage of the new principle of tyre construction led to considerable experiment to produce alternative forms of breaker reinforcement. The most successful of these was Pirelli's 'Cinturato' belted tyre, using a textile breaker band (Figure 13·12). The properties of this construction were less extreme than those of the Michelin 'X', and it found fairly rapid acceptance as a high-performance tyre for sports cars. Subsequent use of the Pirelli design, under licence, by Dunlop in Germany, was combined with the attractive sports pattern known as SP3 Spezial (Figure 13·13).

Truck tyre patterns

In the truck tyre field application of the Michelin 'X' principle, beginning in 1952, resulted in much quicker acceptance on a wide front than was accorded to the car version of the construction. The tyre found favour not by virtue of extra mileage, but because, with its all steel construction, using steel cord in casing as well as breaker, it had a high load capacity for its size.

In England acceptance of the rigid breaker car tyre was relatively slow, and it was necessary to wait for cars to be designed to suit the new properties of these tyres, before they became adopted. Jaguar, Rover and Triumph were first in the field, while the Austin '1800' was the first British large production to appear on radial tyres. At this stage 'The Economist' commented in September 1964, '*British car manufacturers have shied away in the past from buying components at more than minimal costs. They are changing their attitudes fast with the advent of the radial ply tyre, whose greater expense is more than compensated for by better wear and road holding characteristics. These tyres are so different from previous types that the best results are obtained by re-designing cars round them.*'

In the truck tyre field, the time had come to make special tyres for special uses. It was no longer enough to have one general-purpose road pattern and one special cross-country tyre primarily for army use.

What was now provided consisted of two new ranges of commercial tyres, one for specialised off the road use for work such as quarrying, involving continuous operation under tough conditions, where cutting and impact on loose stones were always present (Figure 13·14).

The second range consisted of an in-between, compromise tyre, capable of being used on hard roads as necessary, without developing irregular wear, and at the same time giving good traction and reasonable resistance to abuse, when used on building sites and other off-the-road uses, when making deliveries of material or collecting loads. These tyres, known as 'on-and-off-the-road' types, were introduced into the Dunlop range under the name 'Roadtrak' (Figure 13·15).

CHAPTER 14

Aquaplaning & Legislation

At the beginning of the 'sixties Dunlop produced a new tyre for the 'faster' cars. This was the Road Speed RS5 (Figure 14·1). The Company had experience, dating back over three decades, of making tyres which were intermediate in properties between those of road tyres and racing equipment. In the 'thirties these had been confined to occasional demands for special equipment, to enable heavy powerful European cars to cross India under high temperature conditions, without trouble from tread-stripping.

Road speed tyres

From such 'special orders' demand had increased with the coming of production-line building of fast cars until the Road Speed tyre was a regular part of the tyre production programme.

The RS5 tyre brought together in one tyre several of the design features which have already been described. Thus it had the intensively knife-cut tread of the 'WH2' pattern, a nylon casing (for strength and resistance to high speed), and the safety shoulder developed in the German 'B7' design. The new tyre was rapidly accepted as a tyre of outstanding performance, especially at speed on wet roads, and the pattern had a long run of success extending over many years.

High grip tyres

For a short period Dunlop in Great Britain had a second special tyre on sale. This was introduced in 1960 and named the 'Elite'. This was a very safe and luxurious tyre, embodying all that had been learned about high grip treads and very soft ride properties (Figure 14·2). The claims made for it were that it gave 45% more resistance to wheelspin, 24% better wet hold in cornering and 15% more braking grip. It also eliminated squeal when cornering.

The tyre was produced in a small range of sizes for luxury cars. It had a rudimentary tread pattern, to suit the compound used. It matched the standard tyre in speed capability and it was admitted that fuel consumption was increased by about 2%. The tyre was important as a practical exercise in displaying the properties of the extreme high-grip tread. The rapidly expanding motorway network, which at that time was subject to no speed restriction, led to little interest in the Elite as a commercial proposition.

Now came the time to introduce a new standard tyre with up-to-date properties. This came in the United Kingdom in 1961-62 and was launched under the code name of 'C.41' (Figure 14·3). It combined, in one standard tyre, three new features, all of which produced improvements in tyre performance, which could be experienced by the tyre user. Two of these were concerned primarily with wet road grip. The tyre had a 'WH2' type microslotted tread, with many knifeblades in the mould to produce microslots in the tread ribs. This pattern was combined with a high grip tread, advertised as 'road hug rubber' —it was not of the extreme type used in the Elite tyre but was compounded to give a useful combination of grip and mileage. The third feature was the first appearance of the safety shoulder in a British standard range tyre.

In due course, in 1964, the same principles of design were extended to the radial-ply range, and an 'SP41' tyre, with the same basic tread and sidewall design features on a radial casing appeared, under the slogan 'now there are two kinds of best' (Figure 14·4).

The level of interest in wet road grip, at this time, was illustrated by the results of a competition held at the 1964 Cycle and Motor-Cycle Show.

Competitors were given a list of eleven features and were invited to 'Design a Motor Bike', by selecting the nine most important points. The most popular choice was 'road hug' or 'cling' tyres. 8,000 entrants, or 27 per cent, placed this component first, and a further 16 per cent selected it as second choice.

In the early 'sixties Tom French, Eric Gough and others of the Dunlop Technical team were considering various problems of the grip of tyres at high speeds on wet roads and on aircraft on wet runways.

Tyre properties

Facts about a dramatic falling-off of tyre grip with increasing speed, under wet conditions, had been accumulating in laboratories and research stations throughout the world. With this knowledge came the realisation that high speed tyre grip, in the last stages of the wear

91

of tyre tread patterns, became extremely hazardous, and that accidents could be traced to loss of grip due to causes not hitherto recognised. This introduced the condition which was called aquaplaning.

Aquaplaning

The facts about the grip of tyres at high speeds may be summarised in a diagram (Figure 14·5) which shows that there are three stages. The tyre is almost worn out and is being braked on a wet road, covered with a film of water. On the left the speed is low and the tyre has time to sink through the water film, to expel the water from under the contact area and to take a good grip on a dry road patch. The tyre in the centre is running at high speed. The time of passage of any part of the tyre over the road is now so short that the water is not properly cleared from the contact patch. As a result, a water wedge is formed at the entry to the contact area and this extends under the road contact area, leaving only the latter part of it clear of water where grip can take place. As the speed of the car rises still higher the length of this cleared portion of the contact patch contracts still further, until a speed is reached, as on the right of the diagram, where the tyre floats completely on the film of water and where all braking grip is lost. This is the condition of aquaplaning.

The dimensions involved are as follows: At 60 m.p.h. in moderate rain, each tyre has to displace eight pints of water per second, from under the contact patch, which is no greater in area than the sole of a size 9 shoe. Each gripping element is in contact with the road for 1/150th of a second at a time as the tyre rolls by.

The phenomenon of aquaplaning was first demonstrated on a test machine. This in itself is a surprising sight, with the tyre, carrying its appropriate load, say 800 lb., floating at rest while the steel drum rushes by at 60 miles an hour (Figure 14·6).

Aquaplaning on the road

Having established the laboratory experiment the work was extended to tyres running on a car on the proving-ground. Here, as the length of track was short, and there was no time to wait for the tyre to slow down and stop, the vehicle was fitted with a separate brake control on the front wheels, so that the rear wheels would keep turning and the car would run straight. The aquaplane slide was started by a short front brake application which was signalled by a brake light over the front wheel arch. When the front wheels were locked momentarily they continued to slide in an aquaplane movement over the wet track (Figure 14·7). Close-up photographs and films were taken with cameras carried on outriggers on the car (Figure 14·8).

The driver, wearing white gloves for visibility, could be seen inside the car swinging the steering wheel from side to side as the car slid straight ahead.

Subsequently the same demonstration was extended to heavy vehicle tyres, with even more spectacular results (Figures 14·9 & 14·10).

These two experiments, on machine and track, gave Dunlop a story of the greatest interest and importance to show to the press of the world. Apart from demonstrations at Fort Dunlop the story was photographed and filmed and seen world wide. Nobody having seen the demonstrations could doubt the seriousness of aquaplaning as a problem with smooth or nearly smooth tyres.

It was fortunate that just at the time of this discovery Dunlop had the SP 41 radial ply tyre, ready for launching. The tyre, with its circumferential grooves, held open under load by the rigid breaker structure, gave a complete freedom from aquaplaning, within the speed range for which it was designed, so long as there was a reasonable pattern depth remaining. Furthermore the possession of the testing technique for checking on aquaplaning performance enabled new patterns to be tested at the experimental stage under known aquaplaning conditions, and to be produced with firm knowledge as to what their service properties were going to be.

A further technique which was developed enabled the water distribution under the tyre contact patch to be photographed. The set-up on the Dunlop proving ground is shown in (Figure 14·11). The tyre runs over a glass plate, let into the track surface, and shielded by a large sky-hood. The glass plate is covered with water containing fluorescein, which photographs bright green by flashlight. Below the glass plate is a camera together with electronic flash apparatus, which is triggered by the passage of the car. Some of the results of such investigations are shown here (Figure 14·12), which shows three stages in the advance of the water wedge under the tyre until finally aquaplaning takes place.

In 1964 a new principle of tread design was patented in the name of Tom French. In a subsequent paper delivered in the U.S.A. he explained the field of operation. *'The few square inches of the tyre/ ground contact are where everything starts and finishes. Tyre designers should be trained to get themselves mentally into this arena, to know its complexities in detail and from the standpoint of this subject, very largely to forget tyres in the way we normally look at them, i.e. toroidal rubber*

New ideas on wet grip

93

shapes with their particular structures, design configurations, their styling contribution to vehicles and so on. Everything depends on what is going on down at the ground.'

By using studies published by R. N. J. Saal, it was possible to produce a graph of water film thickness against time, for an elipse similar to that of the footprint of a tyre, sinking through a water film one tenth of an inch thick. As the water film decreases in thickness, the time taken to penetrate it increases. This means that the removal of the last traces of water, from under the tyre contact becomes increasingly difficult.

A series of small reservoirs is needed, to take up the surplus water, and these must be placed in the tread surface, at such intervals of distance that the water can travel to them in the very short time which is available. With a tyre running at 60 m.p.h. this time is about one ten thousandth of a second.

French's patent therefore covered a system of microslots so arranged, in number and distance apart, that the final remaining water could reach them in the very short time available.

The specification describes the function of slots in the tread as now seen: *"It has been discovered that the provision of slots is of considerable value, not only for skid resistance but also by virtue of the fact that the slots operate as local reservoirs which have the function of soaking up water from the portion of the contact area of the tyre . . ."*

This marks a change in thinking as to the way in which knifecut patterns work. Originally the 'blades' of rubber were seen as squeegees, wiping the water off the road surface. Now the slots themselves are seen to act like the cavities in a sponge, in mopping up the last drops of water, and storing it, backed up by the pressure of the air already present in the slot, until the load comes off and the water is expelled.

New designs

The new patent was soon used as the basis for two designs for radial tyre treads, which appeared in 1968. The first of these was the 'SP 68', the replacement for the 'SP.41' (Figure 14·13). The increase in the density of knife-cutting in the tread surface will be seen at once. This marked the tyre as being recognisably different from anything that had been available before.

Publicity was concentrated on the 'magic carpet ride'. The extra flexibility which the closely-packed slots in the tread gave was described as the 'Velflex tread'. This illustrated once more that all

94

the properties of a tyre are interlocked and that a modification of one property will immediately react on others. In this case high-density grip-slots were added to the tread; primarily to increase wet-grip. As a by-product we find that we have a tread of exceptional flexibility, with a caterpillar-like capacity to adapt itself to the features of the road surface.

The properties of the new tyre were checked by photography in action through the glass road (Figure 14·14). The fact that the micro-slots are all full of water and are really mopping up the contact area can be clearly seen.

Other features of the SP 68 pattern included a wider profile and a squarer shoulder to shoulder contact area. This gave a 20-30% increase in mileage, compared with the earlier SP41, provided, of course, that the improved cornering properties were not too vigorously exploited.

The other tyre, produced at about the same time, was the 'SP-Sport' (Figure 14·15). The tread treatment was similar to that of the SP 68 already described. But the 'SP Sport' included two other features, to give improved drainage of the bulk water, in the early stages of taking a grip on the road.

The obvious feature is the wide, unobstructed centre channel. But at the sides of the pattern there are new features, known as aquajets, designed to convey water away from the sidegrooves of the pattern. These consisted of tunnels, through the sideribs of the tread, which enabled water to be ejected sideways as the tyre rolled under load. Photographs, taken through the glass road and from an outrigger above the road surface, show these aquajets in action (Figures 14·16 & 14·17).

One feature of tyre design, which underwent significant change during the 'sixties, was the ratio of height to width of tyre section. The following is a summary of the stages by which tyres became squatter in section.

Tyre profiles

The early tyres were roughly circular in section, with height 100% of width, e.g. 5.25-16 etc.

The cushion type range of cross-ply tyres saw the ratio reduced to 95%, e.g. 5.60-13 etc.

The medium profile range was based on a ratio of 88%, e.g. 6.00-13 etc.

Next came a Low Profile range, at 82% ratio, this included a number of metric cross-ply sizes and such fundamental radial sizes as 165-15.

The '70' series saw the 70% height to width ratio used as the name of the range. It includes such cross-ply sizes as B70-14 etc, and radials such as 165/70SR13 and DR70SR14.

Moves to reduce the height/width ratio below 70% followed, and sizes in a 60% range became established on an experimental basis, and became part of the range in 1980. In the field of racing the practice was carried to extremes and ratios as low as 30% were used.

The objective of this trend towards lower tyre sections is to put more tread on the road, give more lateral stability, better road-holding and longer life.

It happens too that advanced radial constructions are better adapted to construction in a low profile shape than they would have been in sections of greater height.

The 'SP' range of tyres attracted considerable interest and attention, with its combination of radial casing properties less extreme than those of Michelin's original 'X', together with highly sophisticated pattern developments.

The original German 'SP 3' tyre became highly regarded in the rally and trials field, and was much sought after by the sports car drivers of the world. 'We advertise it—you bloody well try to get it!', said a Dunlop Sales Director, at a time when the demand was high and the stocks negligible.

The subsequent production of the 'SP.41' which was a radial version of the 'C.41' produced tangible recognition in various forms.

Rewards

It began on a purely domestic note, with the award of the internal Baillieu Trophy, 'for outstanding contributions to the competitiveness of Dunlop', to the Technical Departments, world wide, under the leadership of H. W. Badger, Group Technical Manager. This took place at a world Technical Managers' conference in March 1966.

The citation read: 'To have become world leaders in radial ply tyres as well as cross ply is a substantial victory in the long, unceasing struggle. It says much for the imagination and persistent hard work of a host of engineers and production men, of salesmen and research scientists throughout the world. But the success has its origins in Tyre Technical on whom the Baillieu Trophy is conferred in the full knowledge that the award can bring gratification but never contentment.'

Figure 14.1, right
The Dunlop Road Speed 'RS5'
high speed road tyre.

Figure 14.2, left.
The Dunlop 'Elite' tyre with high
grip and very soft ride.

Figure 14.3, left.
The Dunlop 'C41' tyre, introduced in 1961-62, with heavily slotted pattern, high-grip tread compound and safety shoulder.

Figure 14.4, right.
The 'SP41' tyre of 1964, which extended the features of 'C41' into the radial construction and gave Dunlop 'two kinds of best'.

Figure 14.5.
The background of aquaplaning.
The diagram shows the three stages
of loss of grip, as speed increases,
with a smooth tyre running on a
road covered with a continuous
film of water.

In the first stage, at low speed,
the tyre has time, as it rolls, to sink
through the water film, so that full
contact is achieved between the
tread rubber and the road surface,
and grip is at a maximum.

As the speed is increased the
time during which any part of the
tread is in the contact area is
decreased and is insufficient for
complete clearance of the water
from the road. The water wedge
extends under the contact patch
and the grip of the tyre on the road
is correspondingly decreased.

Finally, at high speed, the time
of contact is too short for any water
clearance to take place and the
water wedge extends completely
under the contact patch. The tyre
then fails to secure any effective
grip on the road and the car
aquaplanes.

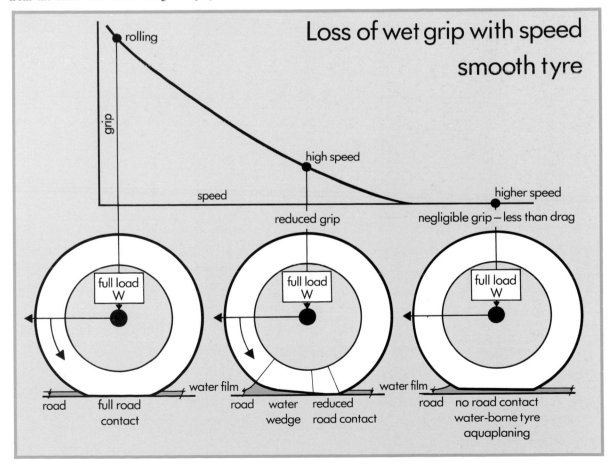

Figure 14.6, top.
Aquaplaning on the test machine. The smooth tyre is stationary and capable of being turned by hand, although the drum is rotating at 60 m.p.h. and a load of 800 lb. is being carried.

Figure 14·7, centre.
Aquaplaning on the test track. The smooth tyres on the front wheels slide on the water film on the track, at 60 m.p.h. The car remains stable since the patterned rear tyres are still rotating and gripping the track.

Figure 14.8, below.
Closeup taken from an outrigger, showing a smooth tyre with a water-wedge built up in front of the contact patch while the tyre aquaplanes without any grip.

Figure 14.9, top.
Aquaplaning on a worn truck tyre on the test machine.

Figure 14.10, below.
Heavy truck aquaplaning on the wet track on smooth front tyres.

Figure 14.11
Jaguar car crossing glass plate let into road. The footprint of the tyre is photographed by a camera below the road, with electronic flash which is triggered by the passage of the car.

Figure 14.12, below.
Photographs taken through the glass road, in the wet.
A. (left) at 30 m.p.h. the area of tread to road contact is still adequate.
B. (centre) at 40 m.p.h. the tread contact is decreasing as the water wedge advances.
C. (right) at 60 m.p.h. there is no time for the tyre to clear the road of water, contact is lost and aquaplaning takes place.

Figure 14.13
Dunlop SP 68 pattern, with high density knife slotting in the tread surface of a radial ply tyre.

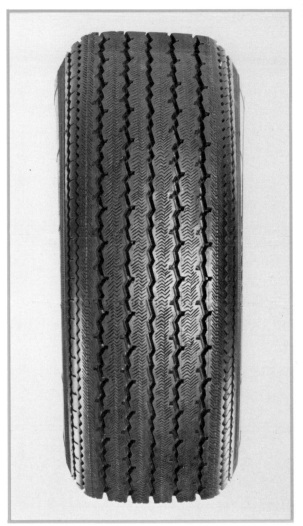

Figure 14.14
The footprint of the SP 68 pattern, photographed at speed, in the wet, through the glass road, showing excellent water dispersion and the high proportion of dry-road contact which is achieved.

Figure 14.15, left.
Dunlop 'SP Sport' tyre of 1968-69. The tyre has tunnels moulded through the outer ribs of the tread pattern, shown enlarged in the inset. Through these water from the road surface is ejected in 'aquajets' as the tyre runs, increasing the efficiency of the pattern in securing road grip.

Figure 14.16, below left.
The 'SP Sport' tyre photographed by high speed flash through the glass road, showing the excellent water clearance and the aquajets in action.

Figure 14.17, below.
The tyre photographed at speed from an outrigger mounted on the car.

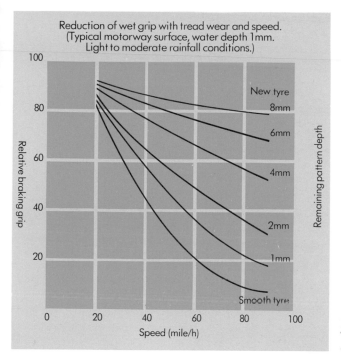

Figure 14.18
The effect of tread wear on braking
efficiency during light rain.

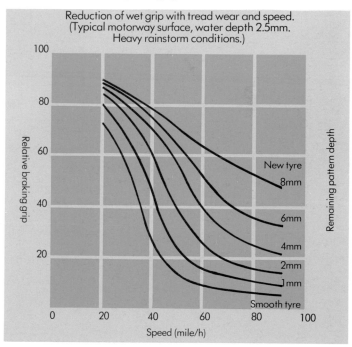

Figure 14.19
The effect of tread wear on braking
efficiency during heavy rain.

Test 1	RB.6	Highway P.T.
Vehicle	A	B
Distance rolled	880ft.	640ft.
Test 2		
	B	A
Distance rolled	1142ft.	826ft.
Advantage to RB.6	Test 1	80yds
	Test 2	105yds

Figure 14.20
Results of comparisons made on a double-deck vehicle equipped in turn with Dunlop RB6 radial tyres and corresponding cross-ply equipment, and allowed to roll freely down an incline.

Figure 14.21
Comparison of the RB6 radial-ply with cross-ply tyres, in a test in which a double deck vehicle was towed up a slight incline, with a dynamometer measuring the pull in the tow-bar.

Vehicle	Midland Red bus	Ballast plus 16 passengers
		Gross vehicle weight – 10¼ tons
Tyres	10.00–20 RB.6	10.00–20 Highway P.T.
	Front 85 psi Rear 65 psi	Front 85 psi Rear 65 psi Actual service condition
Number of passengers carried	16	2
Draw bar pull	710 lbs	700–710 lbs
14 extra passengers carried for the same draw bar pull when RB.6 tyres are fitted.		

Figure 14.24, right
The radial giant tyre with full depth
knife slots.

Figure 14.22
The Highway 70 pattern, with up-
dated grip properties on wet roads.

Figure 14·23, below.
Reducing the gap between the
stopping distances on wet slippery
roads of the modern car tyre and
the tyres used on commercial
vehicles. The chart shows the 33%
improvement in stopping distance
on truck tyres achieved by a redesign of the tread. It also
illustrates the even closer approach
to car tyre properties which is
possible in tyres for Light Trucks.

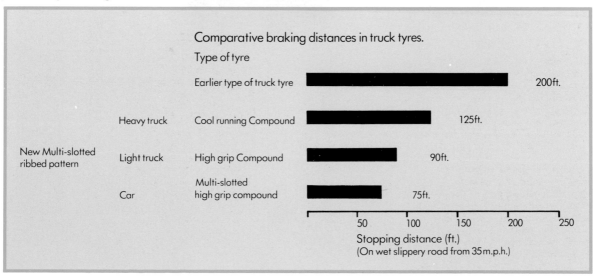

Comparative braking distances in truck tyres.

Type of tyre

		Type of tyre		
		Earlier type of truck tyre		200ft.
	Heavy truck	Cool running Compound		125ft.
New Multi-slotted ribbed pattern	Light truck	High grip Compound		90ft.
	Car	Multi-slotted high grip compound		75ft.

50   100   150   200   250

Stopping distance (ft.)
(On wet slippery road from 35 m.p.h.)

	1955	1970	
	B5	C41	radial SP41
Pattern	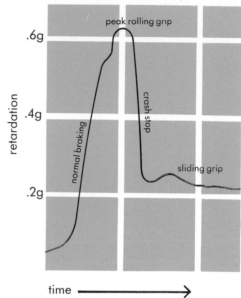		
Tread	high n.r.	high mu	
Tread Life	100	110+	180
Wet Hold			
a. tractive	100	130	145
b. cornering	100	155	170
c. braking	100	125	140
Anti-Wander	100	150	very large
Anti-Squeal	100	200	180

Braking on Wet Road

from 60 m.p.h. smooth road modern tyre new state.

retardation — .6g, .4g, .2g

peak rolling grip

normal braking

crash stop

sliding grip

time ⟶

Figure 15.1, above
A record of fifteen years of technical improvement in tyre safety.

Figure 15.2, right.
The Standby spare wheel and tyre, 1959, taking up minimum space in the boot. The tyre is stored deflated, as in the centre. On inflating, with a gas cartridge, it assumes the shape shown on the right, and replaces the conventional tyre on the left.

Figure 15.3, above right.
Braking graph for modern high-grip tyre, showing the very high peak retardation which can be achieved in normal braking, up and down the left-hand limb of the graph. Wheellocking leads to great loss of braking effort, as illustrated on the right hand side of the diagram.

In June of the same year, 1966, the Automobile Association celebrated its Diamond Jubilee. Among the first of the Silver Medals awarded to mark this occasion was one to Dunlop for research work in the field of safety. The citation in this case read:

The A.A. Committee was impressed with the amount of detailed research and development work successfully undertaken by the Company in the field of road safety, investigations into braking problems and the development of tyres generally and the SP range in particular.

On the continent the interest in the new tyres was high. Thus at the Frankfurt Motor Show in 1967 the Dunlop stand had a demonstration of aquaplaning, neatly presented on a machine enclosed in a glass case. This attracted so much attention that, at times, the show authorities asked that the display should be suspended, because the crowds were blocking the gangways.

A year later, at the Leipzig International Spring Fair, in 1968, the Dunlop 'SP Sport' tyre, with the aquajets, was awarded a Gold Medal and Diploma.

The 'sixties saw great concentration of interest in making motoring safer. In the U.S.A. legislation was drafted on a wide front, affecting the structure of the vehicle and the performance of its key components, and a beginning was made on the introduction of safety measures and requirements.

Safety regulations

In the United Kingdom the rudimentary beginnings of safety legislation, contained in The Motor Vehicles (Construction and Use) Regulations, were brought up to date and their scope so far as tyres were concerned widened and made more precise.

As from April 1968 these broad requirements came into effect:

The 1mm limit

PATTERN DEPTH—Tyres must have a depth of pattern of at least 1 mm over at least ¾ of the breadth and round the whole circumference of the tread.

SUITABILITY—All tyres on a given vehicle must be:
adequate for its speed, adequate for the load, compatible with the other tyres.

INFLATION PRESSURE—The tyres must be inflated to a pressure suitable for the use to which the vehicle is being put.

DAMAGE—The tyres must be free from damage
a. breaks or cuts deep enough to reach the casing cords.
b. lumps or bulges caused by separation or partial structural failure.
c. exposure of the ply or cord structure.

97

There can be no doubt that these Regulations have been helpful in drawing the attention of motorists to the need to take elementary precautions about the condition of the tyres on their vehicles. But many tyres in the stacks of replaced covers at garages and tyre depots are still seen to have been worn past the 1 mm. limit on tread pattern depth, although there is no doubt that it is appreciated that a smooth tyre is outside the requirements of the law.

It is interesting to look at the technical evidence which led to the setting of the 1mm limit on pattern depth. Dunlop's Technical Department provided themselves with sets of tyres, worn to various stages in the pattern depth. The braking grip of each set was measured, under two conditions of water depth, on the proving ground. The results are shown in Figures (14·18 & 14·19).

The first set of results, with 1 mm of water on the road surface, equal to normal rain conditions, shows that at 60 m.p.h. the tyre with 1 mm of pattern remaining has only 40% left of the low-speed grip of a new tyre.

In the second graph we have 2.5 mms of water (1/10″) on the track, which represents heavy rainstorm conditions. The situation is now much worse, and at 60 m.p.h. the set of tyres with 2 mms of pattern left is down to a mere 24% of its maximum new tyre grip.

These results were discussed with the Ministry of Transport and the various sets of tyres were loaned to the Road Research Laboratory, who repeated the experiments for themselves and confirmed the findings. It was on this basis that the limit of 1 mm pattern depth was decided upon. This lined up generally with European practice, but is less safe than the 1/16″, or 1.6 mm, which is enforced as the minimum tread depth for worn tyres in America.

On the question of suitability and compatibility, enough data is usually available, moulded on the tyre wall, to avoid the use of tyres of different sizes, although they are still found on old cars which draw supplies from the breakers yards. Speed capabilities are shown by a speed rating marking, in the sizes fitted to cars where this is important. With heavy vehicle tyres the permissible load is identified by a ply-rating system, which is also moulded on the tyre wall, and which demands only that like shall be always replaced by like.

Finally, on the question of compatibility, the matter of mixtures of radial and cross-ply tyres on cars must be mentioned. For stability and understeer a car must run with a large slip angle on its front tyres, relative to that obtaining at the rear. Radial tyres produce the needed cornering forces at a smaller angle than is needed with cross-ply covers. Hence if two tyres of each type are fitted to a car, then the radials must go on the rear axle, even if the car has front wheel drive. The law also looks askance at mixtures of cross-ply and radial ply covers on the same axle. Goods vehicles on twin rear tyres at the rear are not sensitive to steering forces in the same way as cars, and usually the fitment of radial and cross ply equipment is subject to less critical restrictions.

Work on truck tyres in the 'sixties was concentrated on the improvement of tread patterns and the development of the radial tyre. These two lines of attack were pursued concurrently and the results were interconnected.

Truck tyres

Early in the decade there was considerable interest in the transport field in the fuel economy properties of the radial tyre. A demonstration was given at Fort Dunlop, to interested parties, which covered not only mileage run on measured amounts of fuel, but also convincing visible evidence of the superiority of radial tyres, as shown by rolling distances down a slope and by drawbar-pull measurements on towed vehicles (Figures 14·20 & 14·21).

The truck tyre designer began to reduce the gap which had opened up between his product and the advanced designs in car tyres. In particular he paid attention to the grave danger of the heavy vehicle, in a motorway situation, being hemmed in by high-speed cars, which could be braked more efficiently than his truck. Such tread designs as the Dunlop Highway 70 (Figure 14·22) were evolved, with the aim of reducing the handicap which was imposed on the heavy vehicle, and had achieved a considerable advance in braking properties.

The demonstrations included full scale aquaplaning on trucks on smooth tyres and proof that the new tyres could reduce stopping distances, at 30 m.p.h. from 200 feet to 125 feet (Figure 14·23).

In 1969 the radial giant was given a new tread pattern, with full-depth knife slots in the centre bars of the pattern, so that wet grip was maintained through the whole of the tread life of the tyre.

This tyre had been developed over a period of years and its performance confirmed by comprehensive testing on a world-wide scale (Figure 14·24).

99

CHAPTER 15

The Seventies

The pneumatic tyre entered the 'seventies in a state of technical development and improvement such as would have been thought next to impossible at the end of World War II. These improvements had been achieved basically due to the development of a sound technical understanding of the science behind the functioning of tyres. In this field Dunlop was fortunate in the work of its fundamental scientists, and in the possession of men who were able to develop the knowledge gained in many fields into commercially attractive products.

Technical papers by Dunlop men were welcomed in conferences of scientific societies all over the world, in America, Russia and everywhere between.

The strength of Dunlop's position was always that the basic technical theory, sometimes difficult to grasp and often without obvious application, was quickly appreciated by practical and forward-looking minds, and was soon expounded to the vehicle engineer, in his terms, and to the ordinary motorist in language which made sense to him too.

Dunlop & development

Dunlop were able, in this way, to consolidate a reputation as the Company with the practical new ideas.

The advance in car tyre safety, from the mid 'fifties to the beginning of the 'seventies is summarised in (Figure 15·1). The total advance shown would have been unimaginable in 1955. The series of small steps by which it was achieved represent a succession of attacks on current limited objectives, each one accomplished and then built upon in its turn.

Ordinary motorists, especially those young people who drive with least appreciation of the risks which they are taking, have no idea how much safer their tyres are today than those of fifteen or twenty years ago.

100

It is unusual, today, for the ordinary motorist to have to lock his wheels. Modern tread compounds and patterns enable all normal braking to be carried out without wheel-locking and with considerably greater control than in the old brake-slide and tyre-squeal days. Many drivers of workaday family cars will be able to remember, clearly and precisely, the last time that they found it necessary to brake so hard that the wheels locked, recalling the precise occasion by its very unusualness.

The graph (Figure 15·2) illustrates the high grip of the modern tyre and the penalty in reduction of grip which follows if the braking is taken to the extent of locking.

Michelin, who first marketed a radial-ply car tyre, continued right through their huge output of these tyres world wide, to use steel breakers with a textile casing. There have been modifications in tread design and in actual breaker arrangements, but the Michelin 'X' family of car tyres has continued to present a tread braced with a steel belt.

Radial tyre breakers

The steel-breaker patents were licensed to other tyre makers. Uniroyal, who acquired the Belgian Englebert company, took over their process and patents on a similar steel-reinforced construction.

The other major tyre manufacturers in Europe tended to use textile breakers, first on account of the patent restrictions which were in force, until Michelin's rights expired in the mid 'sixties after a short extension of time to compensate for difficulties in getting their production established in the immediate post-war years.

Such tyres as the Pirelli 'Cinturato', with Dunlop's 'SP' and other tyres made under Pirelli's licence, used textile breaker structures. These gave less sudden and more controlled breakaway, when cornered to the limit, and had the additional advantage that they could be used on existing cars of earlier design.

To offset these advantages in handling, the textile breaker tyre had a disadvantage, in that it failed to deliver quite as great an increase in mileage as did the steel-breaker tyre.

As a result there has been a change-over by many manufacturers to the use of steel-breakers, for the increased mileage, and this has coincided with the redesign of cars, so that they have suspensions and steering properties which match up with those of the steel-breaker tyre construction.

There was considerable experimentation in the field of new casing and breaker materials. Rayon and nylon were replaced by polyester (terylene) in casings. Glass fibre was tried out in place of steel for breakers. Neither of these changes produced any reaction from the ordinary motorist. There was nothing to be seen which indicated that the new tyres were any different from the older ones. The original material gave perfectly satisfactory service, so there could be no improvement to score up for the new one. The advertising of such changes was therefore unproductive either of enthusiasm or of new business. The replacement of one good component by another of the same calibre produces no interest whatever.

Dropping the spare wheel

The car manufacturers' drawing offices have been asking for years to be relieved of the need to include a spare wheel in the equipment of their vehicles. Weight and three inches on vehicle length could be saved, they say, if the spare wheel could be dropped from the average car, without loss in luggage capacity.

Of course the ordinary motorist, who carries nothing in the boot for most of the life of his vehicle, is embarrassed by the bulk of his spare wheel only in rare holiday situations. But with large American station wagons, with three rows of seats, it is a different matter. In such vehicles there is no room for the large spare wheel either on or under the floor, and valuable seating space has to be given up to find room for it.

This situation has led to many experiments in which the spare wheel and tyre is replaced by something smaller, for temporary use only, when a puncture occurs.

We can pass over the aerosol cans of puncture sealant which so often result in abject failure in the hands of the ordinary motorist, whose punctures are seldom of the regulation size and shape for such treatment, and whose tyres fall off their rim seats and refuse to be reseated by the blast from the aerosol can.

Temporary wheels, with very small section tyres, such as the Dunlop 'Standby' of 1959 (Figure 15·3) have been suggested. Incredible collapsed tyres, distended when required by bottled-gas cartridges, have been fitted to some of the more difficult American cars, where they travel around, waiting for the chance to show if they still work or not when needed. If they do inflate successfully they usually infringe the United Kingdom legal requirements that all tyres on a car should be compatible with each other and similar in properties.

All of these small-size spare wheel solutions of the problem leave the car user with the problem of what to do with the bulky punctured wheel and tyre, when it has been replaced with the special spare.

There have also been many attempts to eliminate the puncture difficulty, by filling the tyre with rubber foam and other materials. The use of natural sponge and horsehair as possible fillers, in inflated tyres was included in Thomson's 1845 patent, as noted in Chapter 1.

Some of the more recent developments in this direction have used foam generated by chemical reaction in the fitted tyre, inflated internally by the gases evolved and hopefully remaining so during the life of the tyre. These methods of achieving a puncture-proof system are heavy, expensive and generally restricted to use at low speed, for instance in quarry work, in which they can be run without overheating and the inevitable looseness failures which would result.

CHAPTER 16

Denovo & The Future

There have been many occasions in the history of the pneumatic tyre when fresh inventions have been devised to extend the scope and practicability of the device. Some of these have been the result of clearly-seen short term needs, others have stemmed from the growth of new types of vehicle or from the availability of new kinds of material for tyre construction. A few have been far more fundamental.

Reappraisal
The beginning of the 'seventies saw Dunlop weighing up the needs of the motorist, to determine what had to be done next to make his travel safer and more reliable. This involved a look into areas which had not previously been completely explored and which, to the necessity-ridden mother of invention, would have seemed impossible.

From the earliest days punctures had been a source of delay and danger. A study was made to investigate the true facts of the matter and to act as a guide to what had to be done. The result was to establish clearly the place of the puncture in the operating field of tyres.

It was found, for example, that 25 per cent of the spare wheels, carried on cars running on the road, were themselves punctured or deflated, or that the necessary jacks and wheel-nut spanners were missing. It was also found that 75 per cent of women motorists regarded changing a wheel on a car as a task beyond their capabilities.

Puncture dangers
The background investigation of the results of tyre deflation on cars gave the clearest indication of the dangers of the failure of a rear tyre. (Figure 16·1) comes from a paper to the Forensic Science Society, and shows the extreme dangers of deflated tyres, which are so often followed by oversteer and loss of control.

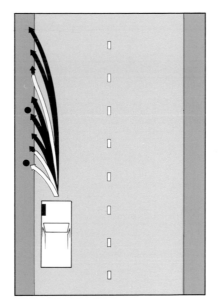

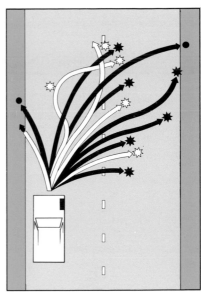

Figure 16.1
What happened after tyre deflations in 61 accidents where it was certain that the deflation took place before and not as a result of the accident.

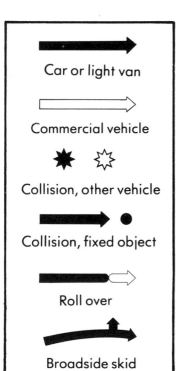

Car or light van

Commercial vehicle

Collision, other vehicle

Collision, fixed object

Roll over

Broadside skid

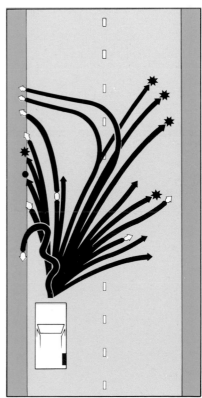

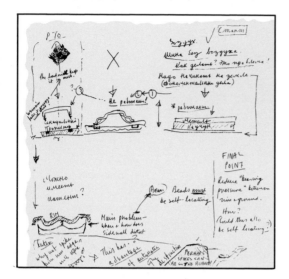

Figure 16.2 The birth of Denovo. The basic idea of the Total Mobility tyre, worked out on a paper napkin in the course of a long air journey. Tom French is a student of Russian and doodles bilingually.

Figure 16.3 Denovo 1. The photograph shows the tyre and wheel, with internal harness carrying canisters of lubricant/inflating agent, on a two-piece, bolt-up wheel. The fluid is released when the tyre runs flat, so that the inner surface of the casing 'fires' the canisters.

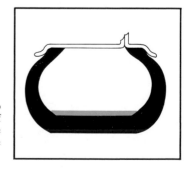

Figure 16.4 The simplified Denovo 2, with the lubricant as a layer of Polygel on the inner surface of the crown of the casing; shown here still on the original two-piece wheel.

Figure 16.5 The Denovo 2 tyre and Denloc wheel.

Figure 16.5A, below right. The Denloc rim. The modified drop-centre rim, with grooves and ridges to retain the beads of the deflated tyre.

Figure 16.5B, below. Tyre on Denloc wheel, showing the way in which the extended and reinforced bead locks in the profile of the rim, when sideforces act on the deflated tyre – (B).

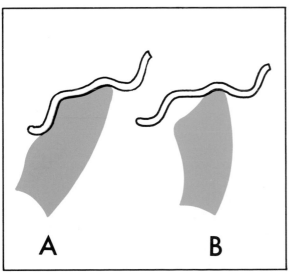

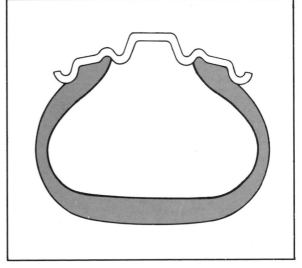

Figure 16.6, above. The Denovo tyre put to the test, Denovo 2, 1980. A Chevrolet 'Chevette' after having been driven from Boston to Los Angeles, a distance of over 5,500 miles, with a rear tyre deflated.

Figure 16.7, above right. The modern motorcycle tyre. The wonder textile, Kevlar, used in a Dunlop motorcycle racing tyre, to give greatly improved casing performance, resistance to impact and other damage.

Figure 16.8, below. The car of the future. 'MOTOR'S' forecast of the family car of 1990, designed by a panel of experts from the Industry. Weight is reduced by 25% compared with similar models of 1980. The tyres are visualised as 150mm section, with 60% height to width ratio.

The increased use of motorways and the high density of fast traffic which they carry, brought a new situation, in which there was difficulty, after a puncture, in finding a way across the inner lanes of traffic on to the hard shoulder, and increased danger in parking there whilst a wheel is changed.

The need was clearly seen for a tyre which would not be liable to these disadvantages and which would not cripple the progress of the car when it suffered a puncture.

The design objectives for the new tyre were set out by Tom French, who was Dunlop's Development Manager, Tyres.

New objectives

"A new order of safety in terms of vehicle control following a sudden blowout under practical driving conditions or following progressive deterioration in vehicle behaviour and safety that goes with a typical slow-leak type of puncture.

Having ensured that the motorist survives the loss of air from his tyres, the objective was to give him 'guaranteed mobility' to continue his journey safely, at specified speed and distance, without the irksome or sometimes impossible task of changing a wheel. The vehicle designer can then eliminate totally the inconvenient and space consuming spare wheel and send it to join the starting handle and other now forgotten encumbrances into the strange limbo of automobile history.

It was a prime initial objective in parallel with the 100% assurance of safe mobility, to render the deflated tyre a 'fail safe' component, so that if it were deliberately or inadvertently abused in terms of speed and distance, or by ultra severe driving, its ultimate failure was not dangerous."

MacRobert Award lecture, 1974

Radial runflat

Various areas of knowledge were available to French and his team as they set about the problem of designing this 'fail safe' tyre. Knowledge of the primary stress properties of the radial tyre had to be extended into the flat-tyre-running state. The background here included the design and production of 'runflat' army tyres in World War II, as described in Chapter 12, and more recent work, in the quite different field of motor racing, where Jackie Stewart had tested out bead retaining devices at speeds up to 140 m.p.h.

The team were also skilled in designing tyres 'from the ground upwards', and they had a detailed understanding of lubricated rubber friction, which had come from earlier studies of aquaplaning of tyres

105

on wet roads, as detailed in Chapter 14. The Dunlop organisation, as major producers of both tyres and wheels, was able to adjust the design of both components of the assembly simultaneously, and to carry out co-ordinated development of the tyre and wheel at high speed.

The work on deflated radial-ply tyres showed how, in such conditions, the reinforced tread band remained as a relatively solid hoop, capable of giving forward mobility and providing adequate lateral control forces. The need to hold the tyre beads on their seats and to provide some kind of lubrication inside the collapsed tyre was also realised. French has recorded how the basic details of the problem of the design of the new tyre were worked out, as 'doodling' sketches, on a paper napkin, in the course of a long air journey (Figure 16·2).

Experiments were made with mock-up devices and the first test of internal lubricants gave a promising ten-fold increase in the runflat mileage. A first design was put into test production, using a tyre from an existing mould, mounted on a flat-base wheel, the second flange of which was pressed into position after the tyre had been mounted on the rim. This throw-away type of unit was soon replaced by a design using a two piece wheel, with the two halves sealed by a rubber ring.

Denovo

The main features of the original Denovo runflat tyre and wheel system are shown in the diagram (Figure 16·3). They may be summed up as follows:

The tyre was of radial ply construction, with a low section height, only 65 % of the width.

The *TYRE WALLS* were thick, the rubber compounds used having low hysteresis, so that heat generation was held to a minimum.

The *TYRE BEADS* were designed so that they locked onto the profile of the rim and could not be dislodged sideways even when the tyre was deflated.

A *LUBRICANT* was supplied to cut down internal friction when the tyre ran flat. This was in two forms, the first a gel, coated onto the inside of the crown of the cover, the second a liquid, contained in small cannisters, carried on a light harness on the rim surface. The liquid was released by a pressure valve which was triggered by the crown of the deflated tyre.

106

The *LIQUID* contained two components, one of which was a lubricant supplementing that coated on the crown of the casing. The other component was a volatile material which, when heated by the running of the deflated tyre, which could reach temperatures around 80°C., produced a vapour which provided an inflation pressure of 3-7 lb. per square inch. This system enabled the liquid to be carried inside the tyre until it was needed, without the problems of balance disturbance which exist with free liquids in tyres.

The *WHEEL* consisted of two pressings, which offered greater radial accuracy than was attainable in the normal wellbase wheel made from a rolled strip with a welded joint in it. The rim width was less than with conventional tyres, in order to give the necessary lateral stability when running deflated. The components of the rim were bolted together and the base made airtight by a rubber sealing band, clamped up between the two discs (Figure 16·4). The narrow rim, wide tread and short sidewalls gave a trapezium cross-section, which naturally deflected in a regular manner upon deflation, still allowing steering control forces to be generated in a continuous manner.

The objective set for the new tyre was that it should be capable of 100 miles total use at 50 m.p.h., in the case of a simple nail puncture, or of 50 miles at 40 m.p.h. if the damage had been more severe. **Objectives**

The tyre was shown to the Press under the temporary name of 'Total Mobility' in the early months of 1972, after a rapid development and an exhaustive test programme had been successfully completed. The demonstrations were rapidly extended to include the vehicle industry worldwide, the Police and Government bodies. In the course of these demonstrations over a thousand instantaneous blowouts were staged, under a wide range of conditions, and more than 50,000 miles of flat running was undertaken by independent drivers.

In the United Kingdom the Department of the Environment and the Home Office gave dispensations for the running on public roads of experimental tyres in a deflated condition, and by the autumn of 1973 the Vehicle Construction and Use Regulations, which are the basis of motoring Law on tyres, were modified by Parliament, to permit the universal use of tyres without air inflation, provided that they were appropriately designed and designated. **The Law modified**

107

Tests with the Police, on their fleets of cars used under conditions where punctures could be particularly embarrassing, covered a total of ten million miles, with over one hundred punctures occurring at the predictable intervals. Tyres were run flat after these incidents for seventy to eighty miles, and in every case the required degree of mobility was preserved.

Recognition of the merit of the new tyre was rapid and it was adopted by British Leyland as an optional equipment on the Rover 3500, the Mini 1275 GT and the Princess 1800-2000 series. More recently the tyre has been made available on further BL models and also on Italian, French and Japanese makes.

Recognition

During 1973 a number of awards were made to the Dunlop organisation as inventors of the new tyre. The first was a Gold Medal by the Automobile Association, in their Jubilee Year, in recognition of a major contribution to road safety. Then came the MacRobert award for 1973, by the Council of Engineering Institutions, '*in recognition of an outstanding contribution by the way of innovation in engineering, physical technologies or physical sciences, which has enhanced or will enhance, the prestige and prosperity of the United Kingdom.*'

The Royal Automobile Club also awarded their Dewar trophy to the new tyre, as an outstanding contribution to road safety. Other awards included the Don Trophy, for contribution to vehicle safety, the Italian 'Oscar della Sicurezza Stradale' awarded at the 1974 Turin Motor Show, and the Viva trophy of the Worshipful Company of Carmen.

In April 1977, in his Chairman's Address to the Automobile Division of the Institution of Mechanical Engineers, Gordon Shearer, then Dunlop's Director, Tyre Technical Division, reported on experience with the Denovo system up to that date. Out of 110,000 Denovo tyres put into service there had been 4,500 punctures, with an average of 17.5 miles run after deflation and with complaints of lack of mobility after puncture amounting to less than half of one per cent of the incidents.

During the late 'seventies Dunlop continued to collect valuable information as to what happened when a fail-safe tyre was put into service on a large scale, in the hands of the ordinary motorist. They alone obtained this experience, which was of the greatest value in working out the future of a practical runflat tyre.

The constructional complication of the original Denovo tyre and wheel was simplified by a redesign, known as Denovo 2, early in 1979, as shown in the comparison in Figure 16·4.

The canisters of liquid lubricant were replaced by a layer of gel material — "Polygel", on the inner surface of the tread area of the tyre. This lubricates the deflated tyre and seals small holes. There is now no reinflation, except for a small build-up of pressure in the resealed casing, due to heating up of the tyre during running.

The wheel was also redesigned. An essential basic principle of Denovo is the location of the beads tight against the rim flanges, during all manœuvres, including maximum sideforces with the tyre completely deflated. For years it was thought that a two piece wheel was the only solution to this requirement, but a bead locking system, given the name Denloc, which became an integral part of Denovo 2, made it possible to use a single-piece wheel.

Other designers had tried to hold tyre beads in place with humps on the rim surface. Dunlop's designers turned that ridge in the rim upside down, and combining it with an extended and reinforced toe on the tyre bead, produced a locking mechanism which made it virtually impossible to dislodge the beads during any road manœuvre (Figure 16·5). This became known as the Denloc system.

This locking mechanism can also be applied to tyres of standard construction, so that Dunlop's pioneering work on runflat tyres has produced a safety feature capable of universal application.

The second generation Denovo 2 had all the classical attributes: greater simplicity, (three components instead of thirty), lower cost, lower weight and, most important, greater compatibility with existing tyre designs in production and service. Denovo 2 can be handled using normal production techniques, by any tyre dealer or vehicle manufacturer. (Figure 16·5)

On the spectacular front there were public demonstrations that Denovo really did work. For instance, in November 1979, a Fiat 'Mirafiori' car, with a deflated rear tyre, was driven from Fort Dunlop to the Fiat factory at Mirafiori near Turin, a distance of over 1,000 miles. Even more ambitious was the successful run with a Chevrolet Chevette, from Boston to Los Angeles, in early 1980, also with a rear tyre deflated for the whole distance of over 3,500 miles. (Figure 16·6).

The introduction of the Denovo tyre, and its immediate recognition as a major step forward in car safety and convenience, led to great interest in fail-safe tyres world wide. Various internal support rings and tyres-within-tyres were re-examined by American, European and Japanese designers, while multi-chamber tube systems were proposed once more in France. Catch-bead devices, in which the tyre bead has a hooked extension moulded-on, to engage the rim edge, which were originally devised in the 'twenties to offset fears about the wired-tyre on its well-base rim, were re-invented to meet the re-awakened need of a tyre that could not leave its seat on the rim.

Apart from the safety feature, provided by a tyre which did not lose its cornering properties when it deflated, a major interest of the Denovo tyre to the car designer lay in the ability to dispense with the spare wheel.

'Skinny Spares'

There had already been interest in makeshift spares, of greatly reduced size, carried in a deflated condition in the boot and inflated when needed by use of a gas cartridge. These devices were adopted by many American car designers in the late 'seventies and began to appear in Europe. Although not strictly legal in many countries, since they are not compatible in use with the remaining normal tyre equipment on the car, they were accepted as a get-you-home measure, by motorists who found their cars so equipped.

Car design engineers welcomed the prospect of doing without a spare wheel in future models. For instance, in a lecture given at the end of 1979, Jaguar's Director of Vehicle Engineering looked forward to being able to reduce car length by six inches, without loss of boot capacity, when the spare wheel no longer had to be accommodated. He also calculated the reduction in fuel consumption which would result from the reduction of weight of the car and estimated that if all cars could be redesigned in this way there could be a saving of 60,000 tons of fuel per annum in Europe alone.

Radial advance

The 'seventies saw a rapid changeover of cars to the radial tyre, which became an almost universal fitment by the end of the decade. In the truck and passenger bus field the wide acceptance of the radial tyre increased and the use of such tyres on single-piece drop-centre wheels grew rapidly. By the end of the decade it was being proposed in America that the multi-piece rim should be banned from the roads as an unsafe antiquity.

Tread life of car tyres increased as the change-over to radial tyres

110

proceeded. Mileages of 40,000 became common, especially as many tyre makers adopted steel-braced constructions, and a position was reached where it was seldom necessary for the first owner of a car to have to purchase any tyre replacements during his tenure of the vehicle.

This long tread life of modern tyres was demonstrated by Dunlop when introducing a new radial tyre in 1974. A BL 'Maxi' car was driven by one of Dunlop's tyre designers on a journey of 13,500 miles, through Europe, Asia, Australia and North America, which with air links, completed a tour of the globe. At the end of the journey there was still plenty of pattern left, in spite of the very variable condition of the roads covered. The car was then taken for a second tour over the same route and the new tyre was lauched under the name 'Worldbeater,' with a total mileage 27,300 behind the test set. *The World beater*

Inevitably this increase in tyre life has led to a reduction in demand for tyres, which has not been completely balanced by the increase in the total population of cars over the same period. The result has been the closing down of some of the older tyre factories and a concentration of manufacture, with a reduced work force, in the more modern and efficient plants.

There can be no question of tyre development having come to an end. Simplified constructions result from the use of new materials of improved properties. A new textile, Kevlar, has for instance given rise to a greatly improved racing motorcycle tyre (Figure 16·7).

The idea that a car tyre could be made as a one-shot injection moulding, from some incredibly wear-resistant plastic, continues as one of the wilder flights of fancy.

On a more practical plane, the rapidly rising cost of fuel has focused attention on the improvement of the efficiency of the car and the truck in their use of the reserves of energy available in the world's stocks of fossil fuels. This has led to the setting up in America of a legislative requirement that the miles-per-gallon of their automobiles shall be increased from the 1978 average of 21.6 miles per gallon to 33 miles per gallon by 1985. Some part of this saving will be achieved by reduction in the rolling resistance of tyres, although the proportion of fuel used in the tyres is small and becomes smaller as aerodynamic losses increase with rising speed. It is significant, in this field, that the recommended inflation pressures with new cars American have tended to rise from the once *Reduced fuel consumption*

111

universal 24 lb/sq. in. to figures now usually above 30 lb/sq. in. Figure 16·8 is a drawing of a projected family car of 1990, featured in 'MOTOR' in October 1980. The specification aims at a weight of 1400 lb., compared with 1900 lb. for cars such as the Ford Escort or the Alfasud. The tyres would be reduced to 150 mm section, with 60% height to width ratio, with rolling resistance reduced from 1·25% to 0·85% giving a fuel saving of about 10%.

And so, as the centenary of Dunlop's re-invention of Thomson's tyre approaches, we look backward to the years of development of the root imaginative invention, which still stands unchallenged. As Maurice Olley, design engineer of General Motors Corporation wrote: 'Numerous substitutes can be suggested for the automobile, but none for the pneumatic tyre.'

Index

A-Z

116

TYRE CASINGS & FABRICS

TYRES — PNEUMATIC

TYRES — PUNCTURES & PUNCTURE PREVENTION

TYRES — SOLID

TYRES — TESTING

TYRES — TREAD PATTERNS

A-Z PEOPLE

PAPERS MENTIONED IN THE TEXT

'The Development of the Dunlop Denovo Tyre and Wheel',
T. French, Council of Engineering Institutions, MacRobert Award
Lecture, 1974. *9pp.* Page 105.

'Everyday Inventions in Tyres and Wheels', W. Bond, Institution
of the Rubber Industry, June 1931. *14pp.* Page 64.

'The History of the Pneumatic Tyre', J. B. Dunlop, Dublin, 1924.
103pp. Page 16.

'Pneumatic Tires', H. C. Pearson, New York, 1923. *1,323pp.* Page 38.

'The Rolling Wheel, the Development of the Pneumatic Tyre',
G. R. Shearer, Institution of Mechanical Engineers, April 1977.
13pp. Page 108.

'Tyres and the War', Tyre Manufacturers' Conference, July 1946.
15pp. Page 72.

'The Tyre as a Part of the Suspension System', A. Healey,
Institution of Automobile Engineers, November 1924. *105pp.* Page 55.

'Tyres and Steering', J. H. Hardman, Institution of Road Transport
Engineers, 1949. *19pp.* Page 71.

'The Weeping Wood', Vicki Baum, a novel in documentary form,
1945. *508pp.* Page 28.

'Wheels of Fortune', Sir Arthur du Cros, 1938. *316pp.* Page 11.